Directions
for
Christian Living

DEREK PRIME

'Sound biblical principles, clear instruction and helpful, practical application – vintage Prime'

Alistair Begg
Senior Pastor
Parkside Church
Chagrin Falls, Ohio

Directions
for
Christian Living

An Introduction to Christian discipleship

DEREK PRIME

Copyright © Derek Prime 1986

ISBN 978-1-84550-614-8

Previously Published in 1986
First Published in 1994 and Reprinted in 2010
by
Christian Focus Publications Ltd
Geanies House, Fearn, Ross-shire,
IV20 1TW, Scotland, Great Britain.

Cover design by Paul Lewis

Printed by
Norhaven AS, Denmark

Contents

Preface 7

1   Understand what's happened! 9

2   Know you can be sure! 21

3   See where your strength is! 33

4   Be prepared for battle! 45

5   Make Jesus Lord! 59

6   Share your faith! 75

7   Aim at proper goals! 93

8   Getting to grips with the Bible! 113

9   Learn how to pray! 129

10 Get your focus right! 145

Preface

The most important part of a building is its unseen foundations – its stability depends upon them.

This book aims at summarising the directions the Bible gives for living the Christian life – the foundation truths it provides for Christian stability and growth.

It is intended to be an introduction to discipleship for the new Christian and a stimulus to spiritual growth for the established Christian as familiar foundation truths are brought into focus.

Each chapter concludes with questions. Besides being useful for the individual reader to answer, they may prove particularly helpful as a basis for group discussion, where that is possible.

Nothing helps to anchor biblical truth in our minds more than personal investigation, and for this reason the chapters also conclude with Bible references for further study.

The biblical text quoted throughout the book is that of *The New International Version*.

1

Understand
what's happened!

'Whatever's happened to you?' That's the kind of question we may be asked once we've committed ourselves to Jesus Christ. I taught in a boys' school for three years, and I received an encouraging letter – nearly 30 years afterwards – from one of the boys I taught. He reminded me that he'd been something of a rascal at school and that after university he spent three years hitchhiking around the world, becoming increasingly aware of the purposelessness of his life. In his letter he related how some years later he picked up a Christian booklet while on holiday entitled *Journey Into Life*, and through reading it he had been brought to faith in the Lord Jesus Christ. As a result, his life has been changed for the better – he's different now!

Our lives change radically when we become Christians. Our contemporaries and friends will probably consider it strange that we no longer want to do many of the things we used to do with them (1 Pet. 4:4). Some of our past activities may have been obviously wrong, and others just not profitable. Our direction in life has now changed. Life has really begun all over again for us.

DIFFERENT FOR THE RIGHT REASONS

We should be different people as Christians, and different for the right reasons. I'm not suggesting we should try to be different. We're all suspicious – and rightly so – of someone who puts on a pose and pretends to be something that he isn't. But such an inward revolution takes place when we become Christians that the differences a complete change of management brings can't help but show themselves.

CONVERSION

First of all, we've been converted. Strange ideas exist about conversion. If we say, 'I've been converted', the probability is that people will think we've become some kind of religious fanatic, or they'll describe us as having 'turned religious'. I don't think, however, we should avoid using the word 'conversion', but rather we should show by the real difference conversion makes what a wonderful thing it is.

Conversion means *turning*. On becoming a Christian we turn *from* in order to turn *to*. Paul wrote of the conversion of the Thessalonian Christians in these terms: '[Y]ou turned to God from idols to serve the living and true God, and to wait for his Son from heaven' (1 Thess. 1:9, 10). The *turning from* aspect of conversion is *repentance*.

It's important not to take it for granted that we understand what repentance involves. When I sin I may be sorry for what I've done, and even go so far as to admit it to others and ask their forgiveness, where that's appropriate. But that may not yet be repentance. I may, for instance, then go on to do the same thing all over again. Repentance means more than just being sorry, and it's more than admitting or confessing where I've gone wrong. It's bitterly regretting the very nature of sin – that it's rebellion against God. Repentance is changing my mind about my sin so that I don't only admit and confess it, but I determine not to go that way again where it's in my power to avoid it.

Now we'll probably think immediately, 'I'm not strong enough in myself to see through such a determination.' That's why the Bible indicates that repentance is a gift from God — it's a virtue that He works in us and something that brings a revolution in the realm of our will. And precisely because it is God's gift, it may be expected to be an effective and powerful principle in our life.

The church of Jesus Christ is made up of men and women whose lives have been changed and are being changed by His power. Reminding the Corinthians that 'the wicked will not inherit the kingdom of God', Paul spelt out what he meant: 'Do not be deceived: Neither the sexually immoral nor idolaters nor adulterers nor male prostitutes nor homosexual offenders nor thieves nor the greedy nor drunkards nor slanderers nor swindlers will inherit the kingdom of God' (1 Cor. 6:9, 10). And then he wrote, 'And that is what some of you were' (11). Notice, that's what some of them *were* — they had now been converted, and therefore they had repented — turned away — from these things. When the Lord Jesus conveyed God's forgiveness to a woman who had been caught in the act of adultery, He also said to her, 'Go now and *leave* your life of sin' (John 8:11).

I'm not suggesting that after our conversion, we are no longer tempted by sin or that we don't still fall into sin. We always carry around with us a fallen nature, and sin clings to us like mud. But we no longer *continue* doing the wrong things which characterised our old life *as a matter of habit*. When our old sins raise their ugly heads we hate them, and we know that we must turn from them yet again. Whereas sin once mastered us, we now strive to master it.

So while repentance begins with an initial act, it's also a *daily* activity. God doesn't want us to pretend that we don't sin, but instead He expects us to repent and to confess our sins honestly as soon as we are aware of them, and He promises immediate cleansing (1 John 1:9). That won't lead to a casual attitude towards sin – as some might think – but it will have the opposite effect. The more we confess sin, the more we hate it and want to turn from it.

But repentance is only the first half of conversion. We turn *from* sin in order to turn *to* God, and this turning to God is *faith*. Faith – this trust – rests upon a solid basis. Christian faith isn't vague and airy-fairy; it rests upon essential facts which the Bible makes plain. It declares first that God our Creator has made Himself known to us in Jesus Christ, His Son, as in no one else – and that Jesus of Nazareth was God Incarnate (God in human flesh).

It explains, secondly, that the main purpose of Jesus' coming into the world was that He might die for our sins as our Substitute. The wrath of God, which our sins deserve, fell upon Jesus so that it might not have to fall upon us. This was an act of amazing love – in fact, breathtaking grace.

Thirdly, Jesus was buried and raised to life again on the third day, and He was seen and recognised by His disciples – and they were transformed by the experience. These amazing events of incarnation, crucifixion and resurrection all took place as God promised they would in the Old Testament Scriptures – the first half of the Bible as we now possess it. On account of what the Lord Jesus Christ accomplished we may receive forgiveness and the gift of the Holy Spirit (Acts 2:38, 39).

These facts have to be understood and received: first we need to give our intellectual assent to them. God doesn't call us to faith in His Son without adequate grounds. The four gospels, for example, provide the plain evidence of Jesus' deity, and, therefore, of the reliability of all that He said (cf. John 20:30, 31), especially that He's the Saviour of those who call upon Him to save them.

But we still haven't arrived at the kind of faith which brings salvation. We must believe these truths about Jesus to the point where we *act* upon them, where we personally *call* upon Him. That's why the Bible talks of 'the obedience that comes from faith' (Rom. 1:5). Supposing you visit me in Edinburgh, and you become unwell, and you ask me for the name of a doctor. I tell you the name of my own doctor and assure you of his credentials and ability to help, and you completely believe me. But that won't do you any good at all until you show that you believe what I say by personally picking up the telephone and ringing the doctor, or physically arriving at his surgery and saying, 'Please help me!' To know that Jesus is the Saviour and to believe that He is the Son of God isn't sufficient – although, unfortunately, that's the place at which many stop. For our faith to be acceptable to God we must personally call upon Jesus in prayer and say, 'Lord Jesus, save me!' Then almost before we know what has happened, faith passes suddenly from believing certain truths to believing in a Person and finding that Person to be real! It's a wonderful experience.

Conversion is made up of these two parts: we turn *from* our sins – which is repentance – *to* Jesus Christ as Saviour and Lord – which is faith.

NEW BIRTH

Another way of describing what happens when we become Christians is new birth. It's a helpful picture because no birth takes place without hidden work preceding it. When we're converted, we soon realise, as we look back over our life, that God was at work in us long before we appreciated it. In fact, it was that hidden work which brought about our conversion.

New birth underlines God's necessary and unique involvement in my becoming a Christian. There's one thing with which
I had nothing to do – and that was my natural birth to my
mother and father. I was there all right, but it happened without
my having any say in the matter! Becoming a Christian – being
born again – is essentially God's work. John sums it up at the
beginning of his gospel: 'To all who received him [Jesus], to those
who believed in his name, he gave the right to become children
of God – children born not of natural descent, nor of human
decision or a husband's will, but born of God' (John 1:12, 13).

One of the first people in the gospels to seek an interview
with Jesus was Nicodemus, a member of the Jewish ruling com-
munity (John 3:1-21). He seems to have been genuinely seeking
after God. He was religious, but he had no personal relationship
with God. He claimed to know about God, but he didn't really
know God personally. Jesus came straight to the point and said,
'You must be born again' (John 3:7). He explained that this new
birth is a work of God's Holy Spirit – the Third Person of the
Trinity – a work as mysterious and as powerful as the wind (v. 8).

Conversion emphasises more the *outward* aspects of becoming a Christian: we are seen to turn from wrong in order to turn
to Jesus Christ and to good. But new birth emphasises more the
inward nature of the work God does in us: we are made new
men and women (2 Cor. 5:17) by the implanting of spiritual life
(Rom. 8:2).

New birth and conversion are two ways of describing the
same experience in that they go together: where there's new
birth there will be the change of conversion; and where there's
the genuine change of conversion the explanation can only be
the experience of new birth.

We've come some way then in explaining why we can't help
but be different when we become Christians. God Himself

comes to take up residence in us. Jesus Christ lives in us by the Holy Spirit. Like a shop which changes hands, 'Under new management' goes up over the door or in the window, and changes must be expected. God the Holy Spirit is determined to form the character of Jesus Christ in us so that we bring honour to Jesus.

ADOPTED

New birth leads naturally to the lovely truth that when we become Christians we are adopted into God's family. I've been privileged to share the decision to adopt with a number of couples. One thing has always been plain: they've *wanted* the child they've adopted! While we feel unworthy to be adopted into God's family, the Bible assures us that God wants us – and that's why He's adopted us.

The disciples asked Jesus to teach them to pray, and His response was to give them 'the Lord's prayer', which begins, 'Our Father ...' As soon as I became a Christian I discovered that I could come to God with confidence. The Holy Spirit is given to all God's sons and daughters so that they may have the assurance to cry, '*Abba*, Father' (Rom. 8:15). I would be very upset if my children called me 'Sir', but I delight in their calling me 'Dad' and their taking for granted my complete interest in all that they do and need. Our Heavenly Father is the perfect Father, and He deals with us individually as if we were the only person with whom He had to deal. As the infinite God, this is no trouble to Him – He can do it perfectly.

RESCUED

God isn't everyone's Father. A misconception exists that God is the Father of everyone. But it's not so. It's true, of course, that He's everyone's Creator. Jesus brought the truth right out into the open when He said to some of His opponents, 'You belong to your father, the devil' (John 8:44).

Our adoption involves God rescuing us 'from the dominion of darkness' and bringing us 'into the kingdom of the Son he loves' (Col. 1:13). The explanation of our spiritual blindness and indifference to God prior to our conversion was our domination by Satan, the god of this age (2 Cor. 4:4). His power over us was all the greater because we were unaware of it. The price of our release from Satan's kingdom was Jesus' death because it was at the cross that victory against Satan was achieved for us. All the time we were alienated from God, Satan had us in his grip. But as soon as we put our trust in Jesus Christ, the conqueror of Satan, then Satan's power in our lives was broken.

Jesus Christ is now our rightful Lord and King. We belong to His kingdom. First, He reigns in our hearts as our King – He sets up His throne there by His Spirit. And, secondly, He prepares a place for us in His eternal kingdom and at His second coming we'll enter into that kingdom and enjoy its eternal benefits. Already 'our citizenship is in heaven. And we eagerly await a Saviour from there, the Lord Jesus Christ, who, by the power that enables him to bring everything under his control, will transform our lowly bodies so that they will be like his glorious body' (Phil. 3:20, 21).

We can see now why there's such a continual conflict in our lives. Satan doesn't easily let go of those who have been released from his influence and power. We'll talk more about that battle later, but don't be surprised at it. When I became a Christian in my teens, I mistakenly imagined that most of my battles would be over. While perhaps some were, new ones began – and they continue! The Christian life involves a fight against Satan and his temptations, but it's a *good* fight. It's a good fight because I wouldn't know anything about such a fight had I not become a Christian. And it's a good fight because with the strength of Jesus Christ I may win.

PHILIPPIANS 1:6

One verse aptly sums up what's happened to us, and it's found in Paul's letter to the Philippians. Paul had witnessed the conversion of many of the Philippians when he visited their city (Acts 16:11-40), and in his letter he writes, '[B]eing confident of this, that he who began a good work in you will carry it on to completion until the day of Christ Jesus' (Phil. 1:6).

My cupboards contain a number of incomplete works: projects I've started and never finished. God, quite unlike us, always completes what He begins. In Edinburgh, where I live, there's what is known as 'Edinburgh's Disgrace' or 'Edinburgh's Folly'. It's a monument, in the most prominent part of the city, which was begun and never completed. It was supposed to be an exact copy of the Parthenon, and was built as a memorial to Scottish soldiers and sailors who died in the Napoleonic wars. In 1822, when part of the money had been collected, the foundation stone was laid with great ceremony, but only the base and 12 columns were built – at the cost of £1,000 each. Nothing more has been done! God's work in our lives can never come to that.

What God begins, He continues – and that's been the experience of Christians throughout all centuries. God's Spirit never leaves us. Like a sculptor with his lump of stone, the Holy Spirit chips away at the rough stone of our lives determined to transform us, with our co-operation, into the likeness of our Saviour, Jesus Christ. Satan will always try to distract and hinder us, but the One who is at work in us is greater than the enemy of our souls (1 John 4:4). We by no means see everything clearly at first in the Christian life, but God's Spirit will continually illumine our hearts and minds by the Scriptures, both as we read them and hear them taught and preached.

Our co-operation influences the speed of God's continual work in us, and we must play our part, but God's Spirit will constantly stir us up to co-operate. We'll find our conscience regularly prodding us on to better things, making us uncomfortable about doubtful things – and God's Spirit achieves this secretly and mysteriously as part of God's continuing work. If our continuance as Christians depended simply on us, we would despair. But it doesn't! 'The one who calls you is faithful and he will do it' was the assurance Paul gave the Thessalonians (1 Thess. 5:24), and it's ours too.

CHECK!

It never hurts to check something over to ensure that it's right. We should check out that these things we've described have happened. Have my attitudes to sin changed? Do I daily strive to turn from the wrong to the right? In whom am I trusting? In myself or in Jesus Christ? As I recall my sin, is His cross my sole confidence before God? Do I delight to call God 'Father'? Is Jesus my Lord and King? Are there signs of God's good work in me?

If so, be glad! And don't be surprised if your old friends and your family find you different. Dare to be different! We don't help other people to become Christians by pretending to be like them. Jesus calls us to be like salt and light in the world (Matt. 5:13-16), and the obvious truth about both is that they serve a good purpose simply because they are different from the environments into which they're placed.

In an interview with a married couple who were applying for church membership, I asked the husband to tell us how he had become a Christian. He explained that he'd been ill for several months in hospital. One of the nurses impressed him

over the weeks because somehow or other she was different
– and the difference expressed itself positively in her high
standards of nursing and caring. One day he plucked up
courage to ask her why she was different. She was somewhat
surprised at the question, but she did explain that she had
become a Christian and that she tried to please the Lord
Jesus Christ in her nursing. As a consequence, the patient
became a Christian – and, to complete the story, later the
nurse's husband!

A PRAYER

Lord, I marvel at Your grace in giving Your Son, Jesus Christ, to
die for me so that I might be brought into Your family. Please
continue Your good work in me and carry it on to completion.
Make me sensitive and obedient to the Holy Spirit, and help me
to live no longer for myself but for Your Son. I ask this for His
Name's sake. Amen.

QUESTIONS

1. We've described becoming a Christian in terms of
   conversion, new birth, adoption and rescue. Can you
   add any further descriptions the Bible gives? (See, for
   example, 2 Cor. 5:17 and 1 Pet. 2:9-11).
2. In what ways would you expect a Christian to be different
   from those who are not Christians? (See, for example,
   Rom. 12:14-21; Eph. 4:17-32; 5:1-21).

BIBLE REFERENCES FOR FURTHER STUDY

ON CONVERSION:
Matthew 18:3; Acts 3:19, 26; 14:15; 26:17, 18, 20;
1 Thessalonians 1:9; 1 Peter 2:25.

ON REPENTANCE:

Isaiah 55:7; Hosea 14:1, 2; Luke 13:3, 5; 19:8; Acts 17:30; Romans 2:4; 2 Corinthians 7:9, 10.

ON FAITH:

John 1:12; 3:16; Acts 16:31; Romans 10:17; Ephesians 2:8, 9; Hebrews 11:1-6; 12:2.

ON NEW BIRTH:

John 1:12, 13; 3:3-7; Titus 3:5; 1 Peter 1:3, 23; James 1:18; 1 John 2;29; 4:7; 5:1.

ON ADOPTION:

Matthew 5:9; 6:9; John 1:12, 13; Romans 8:15, 23; Galatians 3:26; 4:5, 6; Ephesians 1:5.

ON GOD'S KINGDOM:

Matthew 6:10, 33; 13:24, 31, 33, 44, 45; 20:1; 22:2; 25:1, 14, 34; Luke 12:32; 22:16; Romans 14:17; 2 Timothy 4:18; Hebrews 12:28.

ON GOD'S GOOD WORK IN US:

2 Corinthians 5:17; Philippians 1:6; 2:12, 13; 1 Thessalonians 5:24; 2 Thessalonians 2:13, 14; Titus 2:11-14; 1 Peter 5:10, 11.

2

Know you can be sure!

Nothing's more important than becoming a Christian. That's not an exaggeration since being a Christian means knowing the one true God, and Jesus Christ whom He sent, and being sure of eternal life (John 17:3). But since that's so, how can I be sure that I've really become a Christian? Isn't it possible I might be deceiving myself?

Our Lord Jesus Christ indicated the danger of self-deception when He warned, 'Not everyone who says to me, "Lord, Lord" will enter the kingdom of heaven but only he who does the will of my Father who is in heaven. Many will say to me on that day, "Lord, Lord, did we not prophesy in your name, and in your name drive out demons and perform many miracles?" Then I will tell them plainly, "I never knew you. Away from me, you evildoers!"' (Matt. 7:21-23). Jesus' intention isn't that we should always be doubting whether or not we are Christians. Rather He encourages us to be certain that we are so that we don't end up disappointed and rejected at the final judgment.

GOD'S DECLARED WILL

Our first encouragement is that God wants us to be sure: His declared will is that those who believe in His Son Jesus Christ should *know* that they possess eternal life. God doesn't want us to be in doubt about it. If we've repented of our sin and put our trust in the Lord Jesus Christ as the only Saviour, then God *has* received us on the grounds of His Son's atoning sacrifice.

We thought earlier of the lovely pictures of new birth and adoption into God's family. When children are adopted, the adoptive parents want them to be in no doubt at all of their welcome and secure position in their new families. God likewise wants us to be absolutely sure of our welcome and eternal security in His family (John 10:27-29).

TWO SETS OF THREE

The Bible teaches that there are three truths about God and three truths about Christian experience which provide us with the proper assurance that we've genuinely become Christians. In both cases, the three truths go together. It may be helpful to think of two three-legged stools. A stool won't stand on either one leg or two – all three are required. These truths I want to share with you are found throughout the New Testament, but one book in particular – 1 John – deals with them comprehensively, and John wrote his letter with this purpose deliberately in view: 'I write these things to you who believe in the name of the Son of God so that you may know that you have eternal life' (5:13).

THE WORK OF GOD THE SON

The first ground of assurance is the work of Jesus Christ, the Son of God. John tells us that 'Jesus Christ, the Righteous One … is the atoning sacrifice for our sins, and not only for ours but also for the sins of the whole world' (1 John 2:1, 2). Our Lord

Jesus Christ turned aside God's righteous anger against our sins by accepting it on our behalf. John unhesitatingly declares us all to be sinners. If we haven't faced up to that sober truth then we haven't yet become Christians. 'If we claim to be without sin, we deceive ourselves and the truth is not in us' (1 John 1:8). 'Sin,' John explains, 'is lawlessness' (1 John 3:4), and we've all broken God's laws. If we test our lives by the Ten Commandments, we have to declare ourselves guilty of disobedience.

But it's precisely here that we see the wonder of Jesus' work and find our assurance of forgiveness. He died at Calvary to be the Saviour we need. His work upon the cross was what we describe as 'a finished work' – it was complete and perfect, once and for all. It wasn't just an accident that He cried out from the cross, 'It is finished!' (John 19:30). What the Lord Jesus accomplished by His death on the cross was sufficient and complete for all who had already sinned, all who have sinned ever since – that includes us – and all who are yet to be born. It was an *eternal* sacrifice – it occurred once at a point in history, but it has relevance and power for all time.

The assurance that we are Christians doesn't rest, therefore, on our good works – salvation cannot be gained that way. Instead it rests completely upon what Jesus Christ has done for guilty sinners. And it's just as well that it does! If my forgiveness and salvation depended upon my works, I would never know if and when my works were sufficient. On account of my frequent failures, I might wonder from one day to the next whether or not I was still forgiven. The glorious truth, however, is that by His amazing death on our behalf, the Lord Jesus has achieved all that is necessary for our salvation – finally, completely and perfectly!

It's a wonderful moment when we first appreciate that the Lord Jesus has done *everything* that's necessary for our salvation. This truth broke into the mind of a young man of 17 who was

later to become a missionary leader. Hudson Taylor, the founder
of the China Inland Mission (now OMF International) was
on holiday from work. His mother was away from home and
(although he didn't know this at the time) was praying earnestly
for his conversion. He looked idly through his father's library
and then picked up a tract and read it. This is the rest of the story
in his own words:

> 'I was struck with the phrase "the finished work of Christ"...
> Immediately the words "It is finished" suggested themselves to
> my mind, What is finished? And I at once replied, "A full and
> perfect atonement and sacrifice for sin. The debt was paid for
> our sins, and not for ours only, but also for the sins of the whole
> world." Then came the further thought, "If the whole work was
> finished, and the whole debt paid, what is left for me to do?"
> And with this dawned the joyful conviction, as light was flashed
> into my soul by the Holy Spirit, that there was nothing in the
> world to be done but to fall down on one's knees, and accept-
> ing this Saviour and His salvation praise Him for evermore.'

God doesn't tell us to look to ourselves for the answer to our
sins but to look to His Son. We aren't to rest our confidence
upon our own works but rather wholly upon the one sacrifice of
Jesus Christ, a sacrifice which is as acceptable and pleasing to the
Father now as it ever was. The first ground then of our assurance
is the *finished* work of Jesus Christ. His work was sufficient for
my complete salvation and acceptance with God.

THE WORD OF GOD THE FATHER

Since the beginning of this book we've been using the Bible as
our authoritative textbook. Behind practically everything I write
there are Bible statements or principles the Bible teaches. The
Bible is the gift of God the Father, a gift He makes to us through
the instrumentality of the Holy Spirit who inspired the Bible

writers. The Bible is God's witness by words to us. John points out, 'We accept man's testimony, but God's testimony is greater because it is the testimony of God, which he has given about his Son' (1 John 5:9).

The glorious gift of salvation, which the Lord Jesus' saving work guarantees to us, is the gift of the Father, *and His word tells us so*. John writes, 'This is love: not that we loved God, but that he loved us and sent his Son as an atoning sacrifice for our sins' (1 John 4:10). The Bible overflows with God's promises to sinners. The most well-known and best loved is John 3:16: 'For God so loved the world that he gave his one and only Son, that whoever believes in him shall not perish but have eternal life'. And others like Romans 10:13 – 'Everyone who calls on the name of the Lord will be saved' – are to be found throughout the Bible.

What's more, the Bible demonstrates how dependable and reliable God is, so that all His promises may be trusted with absolute certainty as to their fulfilment. It's the word of the Father that assures us that His Son died for *us*. It's the word of the Father that assures us that He adopts us into His family. And God never lies (Titus 1:2)! Others may promise and disappoint, but never God! It's interesting that while the apostle Paul could well have written, 'I know *what* I have believed …' he wrote, in fact, 'I know *whom* I have believed …' (2 Tim. 1:12).

We are bound to be challenged sometimes concerning the assurance we declare we have that God has received us. Perhaps someone will suggest, 'Surely it's presumptuous of you to say that you're a Christian?' But it's never presumption to believe what God has promised. The presumption is rather on the part of those who dare to doubt God's Word! One day when Napoleon Bonaparte was reviewing some of his troops, the bridle of his horse slipped from his hand, and his horse galloped off. A common soldier ran and laying hold of the bridle brought back the horse to the emperor's hand. The emperor immediately addressed him and said, 'Well done, *captain*!' As quick as a shot, the soldier replied, 'Of what regiment, sire?' 'Of the guards,' answered Napoleon, pleased with his instant belief in his word. The emperor rode off, the soldier threw down his musket and though he had no epaulettes on his shoulders, no sword by his side, nor any other mark of his promotion than the word of the emperor, he ran and joined the staff of commanding officers. They laughed at him and asked, 'What have you to do here?' He replied, 'I am captain of the guards.' They were amazed, but he said, 'The emperor has said so, and therefore I am.' And he was right! God's word may be trusted more than that of any emperor, president or sovereign. God's Word, therefore, is the second ground of our assurance – the second leg of our three-legged stool.

THE WITNESS OF GOD THE HOLY SPIRIT

The third ground of assurance is the witness of God the Holy Spirit. 'And this is how we know that he lives in us', John writes, 'We know it by the Spirit he gave us' (1 John 3:24). God promises that all who repent of their sin and believe in His Son as Saviour will receive the gift of the Holy Spirit (Acts 2:38, 39). In fact, we can't be Christians without the Holy Spirit's indwelling: 'If anyone does not have the Spirit of Christ, he does not belong to Christ' (Rom. 8:9). To ask, 'Are you a Christian?' or 'Do you have the Spirit of Jesus Christ living within you?' add up to the same thing in that one can't be true without the other.

The Holy Spirit performs a unique function in our lives – He witnesses with our spirit that we are God's children (Rom. 8:16). I can still recall the wonder of this in my own conversion. Beforehand I had no assurance that I could come into God's presence in prayer and no confidence that I could call Him my Father. But as soon as I was converted, I was filled with joy that I could pray and that I could call God 'Father'. It was only later on that I read in Romans, and elsewhere, that this was exactly what is expected to happen because of the Holy Spirit's activity in the Christian's soul. Paul explains, 'Because you are sons, God sent the Spirit of his Son into our hearts, the Spirit who calls out, "*Abba*, Father" ' (Gal. 4:6).

There are occasions when the Holy Spirit makes us acutely and gloriously aware that we are the objects of the Father's love because of our relationship to His Son, Jesus Christ. We're then overwhelmed by the extent of God's love, and we know that we belong to Him in spite of all our failings and sinfulness. That's a marvellous witness of God's Spirit that we are God's sons and daughters. Every loving father delights to tell his children of his love for them, and God does this by His Spirit's witness in our hearts (Rom. 5:5).

THREE TESTS

An important part of the Spirit's witness is the change that takes place in our lives, and this brings us naturally to the second set of three truths. John presents them as three tests to be applied to anyone who claims to be a Christian. Most days of the week we use banknotes. If asked, 'How can you tell if a banknote is genuine?' we'd suggest obvious tests such as the watermark, its size and the signature to be found upon it. If it meets all the tests, then it's the real thing. There are three principal tests to be applied to the life of anyone who professes to be a Christian. If the tests find satisfactory answers, then there's no doubt about the truth of the profession and of the reality of the Holy Spirit's work and witness in the individual's life.

RIGHT BELIEF

The first test is whether we possess right belief concerning the Lord Jesus Christ. 'Everyone who believes that Jesus is the Christ is born of God', John affirms (1 John 5:1). For us to understand who Jesus is, and what He accomplished for us by His death and resurrection so that we commit ourselves to Him, requires a powerful work of God's Spirit in us, as great as the work of God's initial creation (2 Cor. 4:6). It is not something that can be accomplished simply by human intelligence or decision (John 1:12, 13). For us to say, 'Jesus is Lord!' and to mean it is possible only by the Holy Spirit's illumination and help (1 Cor. 12:3). If, therefore, we declare Jesus to be our Saviour and Lord, with conviction, we have a clear evidence of the Holy Spirit's work in us – and it's part of His witness to us that we've been born again.

CHANGED LIFE STYLE

The second test is whether our life clearly demonstrates that we want to do the right thing *as a matter of habit* – what the Bible describes as 'righteousness'. John spells it out, 'If you know that he is righteous, you know that everyone who does what is right has been born of him' (1 John 2:29). Repentance always brings a change of direction, and most of all because we understand that it was our sins that took our Saviour to the cross. We can't fail to hate more and more all the things that made necessary His death for us. Gratitude dictates our new attitude to sins. Sexual immorality, impurity and debauchery, hatred, discord, jealousy, anger, selfish ambition, envy and drunkenness are sins which have to go, without any debate (Gal. 5:19-21). And instead we want to pursue the attitudes and actions which please Jesus Christ, such as love, joy, peace, patience, kindness, goodness, faithfulness, gentleness and self-control (Gal. 5:22, 23).

Before we were Christians, we might not have worried much if we travelled on a bus without handing over our money to the conductor or giving insufficient information about our income to the Inland Revenue, but now as Christians we find the Holy Spirit making us sensitive to everything that isn't exactly right. We find within ourselves an overwhelming desire to do what's right – and that's what is to be expected of the spiritual children of the righteous God! The evidences of this changed life style constitute part of the essential witness of the Holy Spirit that we've been born into God's family.

It's helpful to think of our lives as a garden and of the Holy Spirit as the divine Gardener. If our lives are full of weeds and diseased plants, then the divine Gardener is absent. But if our lives are flowering with holiness and spiritual fruitfulness then we may be sure that He's present.

LOVE FOR OTHER CHRISTIANS

The third test is whether we love other Christians. 'We know', John writes, 'that we have passed from death to life, because we love our brothers' (1 John 3:14). As soon as we're born into God's family, we discover we possess a unique sense of identity with other Christians. We feel we belong to them as we belong to no other group of people. The family ties of God's family become as close as the ties of our human family – and sometimes closer. The Holy Spirit puts God's own love in our hearts for one another, so that we want to love all of God's people without any exceptions – and that's not a natural human attitude.

As fallen human beings, we tend to live according to our prejudices. We like the look of some people more than others, and so we give them our attention. On the other hand, we may find others uninteresting or even tiresome, and so we give little or no time to getting to know them. But new birth changes that. In every other member of God's family, we are able to recognise our brother or sister; and in each we may discover evidences of Jesus Christ being formed. The first aspect of the Holy Spirit's fruit is love (Gal. 5:22), and all the other aspects of that fruit are the outflow of love. This love for other Christians, therefore, is one of the basic evidences that the Spirit of Jesus Christ lives in us. It also answers one of the common questions non-Christians ask, 'Do you have to go to church to be a Christian?' The answer is, 'No', in the sense that going to church doesn't make anyone a Christian. But the right answer is that on becoming a Christian we love God and other Christians so much that we want to meet with them as often as we can!

BACK TO OUR THREE-LEGGED STOOLS

What I believe and what I know to be true in my personal experience need to go together. I must always check my experience by what God plainly teaches in His Word, the Bible. Knowledge and experience go hand in hand.

I need to understand more and more the wonderful truths the Bible teaches me about God the Father, God the Son and God the Holy Spirit. I'll never exhaust the wonders of Jesus' finished work for me on the cross, the faithfulness of God the Father to His Word and the continuing witness of the Holy Spirit to my spirit that I'm now a member of God's family. The more I ponder these benefits, the more I'll rejoice in my relationship to God through our Lord Jesus.

My assurance increases as I check out my experience with the help of God's Word. But all three 'legs' of the stool must be present. It's not enough to have right belief on its own – the proof of it being right will be its outflow in a changed life style and a love for other Christians. But where all three tests of reality are met, then it's part of the Spirit's gracious reassurances that we are God's children.

DON'T BE PUT OFF

You'll probably be surprised at how unworthy you feel yourself to be to bear the name Christian, and that sense of unworthiness increases as we grow spiritually. The more we know God, the more we feel undeserving of the privilege. Satan, the enemy of our souls, may try to use that sense of unworthiness to make us doubt that we are Christians. The answer is to use God's Word. Turn over in your mind the Scriptures which declare Jesus' finished work and His ability to save the worst sinner. Repeat to yourself God the Father's promises of salvation to all who believe. Remind yourself of the evidences of the Holy Spirit's ministry in your life and the changes He has brought. It won't be long before Satan's attack is repulsed and totally outwitted, because instead of doubting your salvation, you'll be praising God for it!

A PRAYER

Heavenly Father, it is such a privilege to call You 'Father', and I thank You for the finished work of the Lord Jesus which makes this possible, and for your Holy Spirit who enables me to call You 'Father' with total confidence.

May my faith in the Lord Jesus grow and show itself in a life that pleases You and in a warm and practical love for everyone, and especially for those who belong to the family of believers. For Jesus' sake, Amen.

QUESTIONS

1. Why is it important that we should be sure that we are Christians?
2. How would you answer someone who suggests that it's presumptuous of you to say that you're a Christian?

BIBLE REFERENCES FOR FURTHER STUDY

THE WORK OF GOD THE SON:

2 Corinthians 5:21; 1 Timothy 1:15; Hebrews 9:28, 10:10, 14; 1 Peter 2:24; 3:18.

THE WORK OF GOD THE FATHER:

John 3:16, 17; 6:29; Romans 10:11-13; 1 John 3:23; 5:9-12.

THE WITNESS OF GOD THE HOLY SPIRIT:

Romans 8:15-17; Galatians 4:6; Ephesians 1:13, 14; 4:30; 1 Thessalonians 1:5; 1 John 2:20, 27; 3:24; 4:13.

RIGHT BELIEF:

Matthew 16:16; John 6:67-69; 20:31; 1 Corinthians 12:3; 15:1-8; 1 John 5:1; 5:5.

CHANGED LIFE STYLE:

Romans 6:11-14; 2 Corinthians 5:9, 15; Colossians 3:5-14; 1 John 1:7; 2:3-6, 15-17; 3:3, 6, 9; 5:18.

LOVE FOR OTHER CHRISTIANS:

John 13:35; 15:12, 17; Ephesians 1:15; 1 Thessalonians 4:9; 1 Peter 1:22; 1 John 3:10-17, 23; 4:7, 8, 11, 12, 20, 21.

3

See where
your strength is!

'Now that I've professed my faith in Jesus Christ, will I be able to keep it up?' That's a sneaking question most new Christians have asked themselves. Our Christian friends and relatives may cast a sceptical eye on our Christian profession and say, 'Well, we'll wait and see how long it lasts. It may be a seven day wonder.'

If our living the Christian life depended solely upon our own efforts, we might well wonder if we could keep it up, and the scepticism of our friends might be justified. But the Christian possesses a great secret. It's an open secret in that it's not something he wants to hide, but it's something that only Christians can fully understand, and even they haven't exhausted the wealth that it opens up to them. It's the secret of continuing to be a Christian, no matter how tough the opposition or how great the difficulties.

UNION WITH JESUS CHRIST

The Christian's great secret is his union with Jesus Christ. When we were born again of God's Spirit and adopted into God's family, we were also joined to Jesus Christ – we entered into a wonderful spiritual union with Him, the living, risen and ascended Lord. The favourite New Testament description of a Christian is someone who is 'in Christ'. Paul often begins his letters, as he does to the Philippians, with words like, 'To all the saints *in Christ Jesus*' (Phil. 1:1).

IN CHRIST

All that our Lord Jesus Christ did in His death, resurrection and ascension had nothing less than our union with Him in view. First, we were crucified with Him and we died with Him (Rom. 6:6, 8). So complete was His identity with us as our Saviour – in His taking upon Himself all our sins and the awful penalty of death and separation from God, which our sin deserved – that we may say that when He died, we died. The death He died was the death we deserved, and we will never have to suffer death as He did. He has taken the sting out of it. Death will not mean awful separation from God for us as it did for Him, as He stood in our place.

Secondly, we were raised with Christ (Col. 2:12). When our Saviour rose from the dead, the visible proof was given that sin's power leading to death has been broken and that the Lord Jesus is victorious over it. We share His victory, and the Holy Spirit who raised Him from the dead provides us with the power to live a new kind of life. What's more, our union with the Lord Jesus is so vital and intimate that His resurrection guarantees our ultimate physical resurrection too (Rom. 6:5; 1 Cor. 15:20).

Thirdly, we are united with the Lord Jesus in His ascension. He made it plain that He's gone ahead to prepare a place for us so that where He is we may be too – since that's all part of our union with Him (John 14:2, 3). Already God has seated us with Christ in the heavenly realms (Eph. 2:6) – that's where our citizenship now is (Phil. 3:20) – and in the coming ages He's going to 'show the incomparable riches of his grace expressed in his kindness to us in Christ Jesus' (Eph. 2:7). On account of our union with Christ, we've been made co-heirs with Him, and we're going to share in His glory (Rom. 8:17).

God doesn't call upon us to live the Christian life on our own. He has deliberately united us with His Son by His almighty power, and we are meant to live the Christian life depending moment by moment on the Lord Jesus and His strength. The New Testament says things to us like, 'Be strong in the Lord and in his mighty power' (Eph. 6:10). Such a command would be meaningless without the reality of our union with the Lord Jesus Christ behind it.

THE PICTURE OF MARRIAGE

The Bible illustrates our union with Jesus Christ by the picture of marriage, although the illustration must not be pushed too far. Obvious parallels are immediately helpful. On marriage, a wife takes her husband's name. As she signs the marriage register she uses her maiden name for the last time, for she now possesses a new name. When we become Christians, we take Jesus' Name. We are called 'Christians' (Acts 11:26; 26:28; 1 Pet. 4:16), and we publicly declare that we now belong to Him.

Secondly, on marriage a wife enters into the enjoyment of all her husband possesses. In some wedding services, the husband speaks of bestowing upon his bride from that moment all his worldly goods. What's his is now hers. His home is her home, and his life is her life. They are going to share everything together. Similarly, God 'has blessed us in the heavenly realms with every spiritual blessing in Christ' (Eph. 1:3). All that is Christ's is now ours: 'All things are yours ... and you are of Christ, and Christ is of God' (1 Cor. 3:21, 23). His home is our home, and His life is our life (Col. 3:1-4).

In marriage – as it ought to be – a husband's total resources are the wife's to call upon, as often as she needs. Before marriage, she might not have had any money in the bank, but now her husband puts a cheque book into her hands, and she has but to put her signature upon the cheque and his resources are available to her. The Bible is full of promises, and our union with our Lord Jesus Christ is the secret of access to them. All the resources and strength of God are available to us as we ask for them in Jesus' Name (Phil. 4:13, 19).

THE PICTURE OF THE VINE

Our Lord Jesus Christ used the picture of the vine to illustrate our union with Him. He said, 'I am the vine; you are the branches. If a man remains in me and I in him, he will bear much fruit; apart from me you can do nothing' (John 15:5). The picture stresses the vital personal relationship we have with the Lord Jesus. There's no closer or more intimate association than a branch to the vine of which it is part. The whole life of the branch depends upon its connection to the vine – upon its union with it. Cut it off, and it perishes. The life that flows through the branch is the life of the vine itself. Our relationship with the Lord Jesus is as intimate as that, and the spiritual life we enjoy is the direct consequence of our being joined to Him, so that He is our life.

The explanation of our awareness and understanding of this great secret is God the Holy Spirit. God gives Him to us for many reasons, but one purpose – high on the list of priorities – is to make us aware of our union with the Lord Jesus, so that we rejoice in it and experience its wonderful benefits.

SYMBOLS

A union between people finds expression often in symbols. People who are linked together in a corporate body or common interest may wear the same badge, and in marriage the union into which people enter is usually expressed by a ring. The symbol is not the union itself, but it represents that union and may serve to strengthen it. Every time a man wears his badge, he says, in effect, 'I belong'. As a husband and wife wear a wedding ring, they declare, 'I belong to my marriage partner in a unique way that I can't belong to anyone else'.

Our union with our Lord Jesus Christ also has its symbols and two in particular – baptism and the Lord's Supper. One symbol – baptism – is once for all, and the other – the Lord's Supper – is constantly repeated. Baptism is a glorious celebration of our union with the Lord Jesus Christ. As Paul put it to the Romans, 'We were therefore buried with him through baptism into death in order that, just as Christ was raised from the dead through the glory of the Father, we too may live a new life. If we have been united with him like this in his death, we will certainly also be united with him in his resurrection' (Rom. 6:4, 5). Baptism looks back to our union with the Lord Jesus in His death, and it looks forward to our reunion with Him in the future in the resurrection of the body.

In baptism we affirm that we no longer belong to ourselves but we belong instead to our Lord Jesus Christ. The Acts of the Apostles records believers being baptised 'into the name of the Lord Jesus' (Acts 8:16). Those words – 'into the name of' – were a legal formula for the transfer of property. In baptism we declare 'I no longer regard myself as my own, but I hand over my life to be Jesus Christ's, and His alone'. Baptism expresses our commitment to a new way of life – a life to be lived in fellowship with, and obedience to, the Lord Jesus Christ.

In the Lord's Supper we especially recall the truth that is at the heart of our union with Christ – His death for us (1 Cor. 11:23-26). Returning to the picture of marriage, the marriage service itself happens only once, but it's remembered and rejoiced over in every anniversary. The anniversary is the opportunity for looking back with thankfulness and looking forward with anticipation.

At the Lord's Supper we first look back. We deliberately recall the events of that night when our Lord Jesus was betrayed. We use our imagination as we see the Lord Jesus setting His face deliberately towards the cross. We hear Him explaining to His disciples the meaning of the broken bread and poured out wine, and we say to one another and to ourselves, 'It was for us'. Looking back and remembering, we then spontaneously look up to God with thanksgiving.

But we also look forward. The Lord Jesus promised that He would not eat the Passover again until its fulfilment in the kingdom of God. The Lord's Supper is intended to remind us that union with the Lord Jesus guarantees that one day we must be with Him where He is, and that He is going to return so that He may take us to be with Him in His glory. As we eat and drink at His table, we 'proclaim the Lord's death until he comes' (1 Cor. 11:26).

We are not unique in our experience of union with the Lord Jesus – it's the privilege of every Christian. Our union with Him, therefore, brings us into the closest possible union and fellowship with all other Christians. There's but one baptism (Eph. 4:5) – we share it with all other believers. The Lord's Supper – apart from exceptional circumstances – is not something we engage in on our own. We do it with others – it's a privilege to participate in together. It serves not only to help us check out our relationship with the Lord Jesus Himself, but also with one another. We are instructed to examine ourselves, principally with a view to our own participation in a right spirit (1 Cor. 11:28), but we can participate properly only if we are in a right relationship with other Christians. Therefore it is wise to look into our hearts to

examine our motives and attitudes and to look around at our
fellow believers to ensure that we are in a right relationship with
them.

Quite naturally I've used the verb 'look' in different ways in
discussing the Lord's Supper, and it's a word worth hanging on
to when we feel concerned lest we don't obtain from the Lord's
Supper all that we feel we ought. The New Testament doesn't
place the stress on what we *receive* at the Lord's Supper, but
rather it emphasises what we actually *do* as we gather around the
Lord's Table. Rather than asking, 'What should I *receive* from the
Lord's Supper?' I should ask instead, 'What should I *do*?'

Let me suggest that you take this little word 'look' as
a guide. We *look back* – and we remember Calvary. *We look up*
– and we thank God for the gift of the Lord Jesus to be our
Saviour. *We look round* – and make sure we are in fellowship
with those who are joined with us to Jesus Christ. *We look in* –
and examine ourselves and our walk with God. *We look forward*
to the Lord's return, when the Lord's Supper will be needed
no longer. *We look out to the world* – and remember that the
death we proclaim at the Lord's Table we must also proclaim
to the world.

Church fellowships vary in the frequency with which they
meet around the Lord's Table. While the early Christians seem to
have done so every Sunday – and even daily initially – there's no
command in the Bible concerning the frequency of this precious
act. We are not so much told *when* to meet around His table but
rather what we are to do *whenever* we do (1 Cor. 11:26). Just as
every human family organises its life to suit best its circumstances,
so every church has this privilege. What is important for us
personally is to seize every opportunity afforded within our own
church fellowship to remember our Lord Jesus in His death and
to celebrate our union with Him.

OUR UNION WITH OTHERS

Our union with the Lord Jesus Christ is the secret of our union with all other Christians. I can still remember at my conversion suddenly realising how marvellous it was to have so many brothers and sisters in Jesus Christ. I recall the lovely feeling of 'belonging' to God's people. Belonging to the Lord Jesus, we belong to one another. Joined to Him, we are joined to each other.

Most of the pictures the Bible gives of the church have to do with the relationship we have with one another because of our prior relationship to the Lord Jesus Christ. He's the vine, and we're all branches of the same vine. He's the foundation of the building – God's holy temple – and we're all like stones or bricks built together on the one foundation. The Lord Jesus is the Shepherd, and we're all sheep of His one flock. He's the Head of the body, and we are all individually members of that one body. It's our union with the Lord Jesus which makes us members of His church, for which He gave Himself. Our membership of His church, therefore, matters.

CHURCH MEMBERSHIP

We mentioned earlier that the question is sometimes asked by non-Christians, 'Do you have to go to church to be a Christian?' I say 'non-Christians' because I don't think a Christian ever feels it necessary to ask such a question. The answer is, of course, that a person doesn't have to go to church to be a Christian since it's faith in the Lord Jesus Christ that makes a person a Christian. But, at the same time, we'll never meet a genuine and healthy Christian who doesn't delight in meeting with other Christians and joining with them in worship, prayer and service. Church membership is natural to us as Christians because of the family relationship into which our union with the Lord Jesus has brought us.

Church membership is God's important provision for the nurturing of our spiritual life. We were brought into His family through His Word, and we grow as Christians as we are fed by that same Word. To this end, God raises up pastors and teachers who can teach us God's Word and be Christ's undershepherds to us.

Church membership is God's provision too for the discipline we may need if we go astray. Although we've been converted, our hearts remain perverse. We can all make mistakes. None of us is immune from temptation. We may require correction, therefore, and we need to be in a position where appropriate people are there to provide it, and where too – if God wills – we may be able to help others when they need it.

Church membership is the means God has provided so that we may discover, develop and use our spiritual gifts. We've all natural gifts with which we're born, and we're all given spiritual gifts when we're born into God's family and united to Christ (1 Cor. 12:7, 11). But our spiritual gifts are gifts for the body of Christ, and we find scope for their exercise and development only as we properly identify ourselves with the visible expression of that body in the local church. When Christians fail to use or develop their gifts, it's more often than not because they've cut themselves off in some way from other Christians.

Church membership is the principal means by which the gospel is effectively proclaimed in a neighbourhood. The gospel has been committed to us as a trust. We are trustees of the gospel for the sake of those who have never heard it, beginning with those in the areas in which we live. We're unable to cope with such a vast responsibility on our own, but within the local church God provides the unity and diversity of gifts which make the fulfilment of that commission possible. Church membership is a 'must' – but more important still, it's a privilege!

FINDING THE RIGHT CHURCH

It's possible to live in areas where it's not easy to find Christian fellowship. On the other hand, there are localities where there are many churches from which to choose. It's helpful to remember that our situation never takes God by surprise and that He always goes before us. He has already determined the church fellowship where He wants us to find fellowship and to live our lives in harmony, worship and service with other Christians. If you haven't yet found the right church, begin by praying that God will clearly direct you to the place of His choice.

It's important to know what we should be looking for when we visit churches with a view to discovering a spiritual 'home'. First, I would suggest you look for a church where the Lord Jesus Christ and His gospel are clearly preached, according to the Word of God. It won't take you long to discover whether or not that's the case.

Second, look for a church where you sense God's presence and where you feel at home. It's difficult to define what we mean by the Lord's presence – it's better experienced than described! Personally I would define it in terms of being aware of the Lord speaking to me through His Word as it's preached, and of His Spirit bringing God's glory before me through the ministry of His Word and the worship. I would expect to feel within myself the conviction that I'm in a special way at 'home' – that I'm among the people to whom I belong. I know that I belong in fact to all of God's people, but I do have a special awareness too of belonging to a particular part of God's family.

Third, make sure that you are at ease and happy with the practices of a church. We've thought earlier of the symbols of our union with the Lord Jesus – of baptism and the Lord's Supper – and it's important to feel that you go along with a local church in what it believes and teaches about these symbols, since there are varying convictions and approaches among God's people. I haven't put this at the top of the list, however, for if only one church in my area fulfilled the first two conditions, and none fulfilled all three, I would identify with the one where the first two were true. While it's important to have clear views and convictions about baptism, for example, I wouldn't want baptism to be the principal condition of my fellowship with other Christians, but rather my love with them of the Lord Jesus.

To choose to be in easy reach of the right church is an important part of determining the right place to live in an area, when we are in a position to make that choice.

HAVE YOU NOTICED?

I wonder if you've noticed how easily we've moved from considering our union with the Lord Jesus to thinking of our union with all who know and love Him. Our relationship to the Lord Jesus and to His people are virtually one and the same – they are like two sides of one coin. In fellowship with the Lord Jesus, I'll want to be in fellowship with His people. Loving them, I'll be loving Him since they are His body, of which He's the Head.

The Lord Jesus Himself is the secret of my strength for living the Christian life, and through my union with Him I can count upon Him for all His resources. In the way He works, however, He frequently chooses to bring me those resources through the ministry of His people and through the wonderful benefits of Christian fellowship.

A PRAYER

Thank You, Heavenly Father, that far more happened in my life at my conversion and new birth than I realised at the time, or still yet appreciate. I thank You for my union with the Lord Jesus in His death, resurrection and ascension and that all His resources belong to me. Help me to enter by faith into the rich benefits that are now mine and to live my daily life knowing that I can do everything through the Lord Jesus who gives me strength. May I always show my love for Him by my love for His people. I ask this for His Name's sake. Amen.

Questions

1. How would you answer a person who says, 'I'm afraid of becoming a Christian in case I couldn't keep it up'?
2. What do you expect to give to other Christians through your church membership, and what do you expect to receive?

Bible References for Further Study

Our union with Christ:
Romans 6:4-8; 8:17; 2 Corinthians 11:2; Ephesians 1:3, 5:23, 25-27, 30; Colossians 2:12, 13; 3:1-3; 1 Thessalonians 5:10; 2 Timothy 2:11, 12.

The meaning of baptism:
Matthew 28:19, 20; Mark 16:15, 16; Acts 2:37, 38, 41, 47; 16:14, 15; Romans 6:3; Colossians 2:12; 1 Peter 3:18-22.

The Lord's Supper:
Matthew 26:26-29; Mark 14:22-25; Luke 22:19, 20; 1 Corinthians 10:16, 17; 11:23-26.

Church membership:
Matthew 18:15-20; Acts 2:42-47; 14:21-23; 20:28; 1 Corinthians 11:22; 14:12, 19, 28, 33-35; 16:1; Galatians 6:1, 2, 10; Ephesians 4:11-16; 1 Thessalonians 5:12; Hebrews 10:24, 25; 13:16, 17; 1 Peter 2:4, 5; 5:2-4.

4

Be prepared for battle!

I wonder if you're surprised at the news that the Christian life involves fighting a battle? Wherever we turn in the New Testament we find the language of conflict. Not surprisingly it appears most in the apostle Paul's letters since he wrote more New Testament letters than anyone else. 'I labour,' he writes, 'struggling with all his energy which so powerfully works in me' (Col. 1:29). Elsewhere, he urges, 'Put on the full armour of God ... For our struggle is not against flesh and blood ...' (Eph. 6:11, 12). Towards the conclusion of his life, he declared, 'I have fought the good fight ...' (2 Tim. 4:7).

Perhaps you thought that most of your battles were over when you became a Christian, but, in fact, some had only just begun! It's true that some battles you once fought are now over. You are, for example, no longer fighting against your greatest Friend – God Himself (cf. Acts 26:14) – and against your best interests. But your new birth and conversion mark your entry into a new sphere of conflict. The reason isn't difficult to discover. The background to our new birth and conversion is the sobering truth that there are only two kingdoms to which men and women may belong – the kingdom of darkness and the kingdom of God's Son (Col. 1:13). When we become Christians, God rescues us from Satan's kingdom – that of darkness – and brings us into the kingdom of His dear Son. But Satan doesn't let that transfer happen without a fight. Many spiritual battles follow as a result.

Don't be discouraged

It's important not to be discouraged or dismayed by the prospect of this unceasing battle: it's a *good* fight. Paul urged Timothy, 'Fight the good fight of faith' (1 Tim. 6:12). It's a *good* fight because it's on behalf of what is good – you are now pursuing God's will instead of your own and Satan's. It's a *good* fight because you wouldn't know about the conflict had you not been born into God's kingdom. The fact that you know the reality of the battle is one of the proofs that you've really become a Christian. Where there's no spiritual conflict there's no spiritual life – it's as straightforward as that.

It's a *good* fight too because we're in it together as Christians. Believers all over the world experience the same conflict against the world, the flesh and the devil (1 Pet. 5:9), and we are all fellow-soldiers in the same army (Philem. 2). It's a *good* fight because we're not left to fight it on our own: our Lord Jesus Christ is with us, and our union with Him is the secret of our strength to fight and win. And that's not all! It's a *good* fight because it will end in triumph and bring an eternal reward at our Lord's return (2 Tim. 4:7, 8).

Identifying the enemy

No battle can be fought successfully without first clearly recognising the enemy. There's no doubt about his identity – he's the devil. He's known by a variety of names – Satan, the wicked one, the prince of the power of the air, the prince of the devils, the god of this world, Beelzebub, the tempter, the old serpent and the dragon. His many names indicate the varied approaches and disguises he may adopt.

We mustn't underestimate the devil. He's real, not imaginary. He's all the more dangerous because he's invisible. An enemy we can't see is always more threatening than one we can see. The devil tends to be underestimated because he's so often been caricatured. Artists have produced grotesque and ludicrous representations of him calculated to make us laugh. However, he's not someone to joke about. Those who make light of him underestimate him.

Satan attacks all Christians, and new Christians are inevitably a principal target. C. S. Lewis wrote to a friend who had just been converted: 'There will be a counter attack on you, you know, so don't be too alarmed when it comes. The enemy will not see you vanish into God's company without an effort to reclaim you' (Sheldon Vanauken: *A Severe Mercy*, p 102).

While all the devil's modes of attack can't be spelt out precisely, it's helpful to be aware of the most common. He attacks our minds, where he can, by doubts. You may be surprised that I should even suggest the possibility of Christians being plagued by doubts. I admit that some Christians may never experience them, but they are a small minority. The manner in which Satan came at our first parents, Adam and Eve, is described in the third chapter of Genesis. First, he sowed a doubt in Eve's mind, 'Did God really say, "You must not eat from any tree in the garden?"' (1) Then he denied the truth of what God had said (4), and proceeded to follow it up by casting doubt upon God's character (5). In all kinds of ways, we'll find Satan doing similar things. I've drawn considerable encouragement in times of doubt from our Lord Jesus' experience of Satan trying to sow doubt even in His mind about His unique relationship to God. At Jesus' temptation, Satan twice said to Him, '*If* you are the Son of God ...' (Matt. 4:3, 6). Since Satan tried it on with Him, it's not surprising that he does the same with us.

What then should we do with our doubts? First, we should be honest with ourselves about them, and with God. Bring the difficulties out into the open and pray about them. A man with precisely this problem cried out to Jesus, 'I do believe; help me overcome my unbelief!' (Mark 9:24). It was an honest prayer that Jesus understood, accepted and answered.

Secondly, re-examine the evidences behind your faith. Go back to the gospels and remind yourself of the Person and work of our Lord Jesus Christ. In particular, consider His resurrection – the historical proofs of it and your personal experience of the risen Lord Jesus. Recall your conversion and the manner in which God shone into your heart and showed you your need of His salvation and of His Son, Jesus Christ. At the same time cry to God for the illuminating work of His Holy Spirit because faith is a gift of God. God won't disappoint you.

Satan may often get at us through doubts concerning things we don't understand in the Bible. Once again be honest where you don't understand, and tell God about it as you pray to Him. Where possible share your difficulty of understanding with an older Christian and work at resolving it. My own experience is that in the end doubts serve to strengthen my faith as I determine to pursue truth, since God is the source of all truth.

DESIRES

Satan attacks us most of all through our desires, and in particular through our physical and sexual urges. Our body, with all its appetites, often cries out to be pampered. This is an extremely personal and private area of our lives. It's important to view our desires in a true light. Sex is a creation of God and is one of His good gifts. His primary purpose in the creation of sex was the procreation of children. Sexual desire, therefore, is one of the reasons why men and women come together in marriage. To fulfil these sexual desires within marriage is right, but to do so outside of marriage is wrong. Although we may not talk about it – because it's such a personal matter – Satan's temptations frequently centre upon our sexual urge, and some aspects of sex are particularly trying when we are younger (2 Tim. 2:22). Whatever happens don't automatically write off your desires as wrong. They are wrong only when they control you and when you allow them to be used in ways God doesn't want them to be used.

As a Christian you should have a high opinion of the human body and all its faculties, since the body is part of God's creation. The introduction of sin into the world – and also into the human body – means that the body needs to be kept in subjection so that it's our slave rather than our master. As a slave it's a splendid servant; but as a master it's terrifying in its rule. Satan loves us to think that it's impossible to control our bodies – remember he's the father of lies. Part of the Holy Spirit's fruit in our life is self-control (Gal. 5:23), and He gives us His power to that end as we're obedient to Him.

But it would be unbalanced to stress sexual sins and temptations to the neglect of other desires we have. We mention them first in order to be honest and because we can't live in the world without being bombarded with inducements to regard purity as either old-fashioned or impossible. Satan gets at us in every possible way, and through all the desires of our human nature. He's got a great deal going for him in his attacks because we carry about with us a corrupt nature which proves to be a constant source of trouble and distress.

So often we'll feel like Paul when he wrote, 'I do not understand what I do. For what I want to do I do not do, but what I hate I do. ... I know that nothing good lives in me, that is, in my sinful nature. For I have the desire to do what is good, but I cannot carry it out. For what I do is not the good I want to do; no, the evil I do not want to do – this I keep on doing. ... So I find this law at work: When I want to do good, evil is right there with me' (Rom. 7:15, 18, 19, 21).

What Paul describes here as our 'sinful nature' is not destroyed at our new birth, but it's something we need to put to death on a daily basis. We won't get finally rid of it until the end of our earthly life. One of the many exciting prospects of our future salvation is that we'll be free from the actual presence of sin. But meanwhile, we have to cope with it and fight against the temptations it presents, especially as they are encouraged by Satan.

THE WORLD

Traditionally, the Christian's conflict has been described as a battle against the world, the flesh (what we've described as our 'sinful nature') and the devil. That's a fair description, providing we don't think of the world in terms of its people. Our fight isn't against the people of the world but against the spirit and attitudes of the world – summed up by the apostle John as 'the cravings of sinful man, the lust of his eyes and the boasting of what he has and does' (1 John 2:16).

Satan dresses up the world's passing attractions in order to make them appealing and tempting. Under his influence the world tries to squeeze us into its mould (Rom. 12:2) so that instead of living as citizens of heaven and disciples of Jesus Christ, we live with our thinking and ambitions much the same as people who aren't Christians.

The Lord Jesus told the story of the farmer sowing his seed and the various things that happened to it, most of them hindering its growth. He explained that the seed is the Word of God, and the soil is our hearts. Some seed, He said, 'fell among thorns, which grew up and choked the plants, so that they did not bear fruit' (Mark 4:7). He went on to explain that these choked plants represent men and women who hear the word 'but the worries of this life, the deceitfulness of wealth and the desires for other things come in and choke the word, making it unfruitful' (Mark 4:19). It's relatively easy to recognise Satan getting at us through our sexual desires or through our pride. But it's not so straightforward to see his getting at us through material possessions and worldly ambition. They tend to be more subtle. We must be on our guard, therefore, and be honest with ourselves. As gradually as a weed may choke a plant so preoccupation with money and the things it can buy may choke the good effects of God's work in our lives.

COUNTLESS DEVICES

Satan employs numerous methods in his endeavours to spoil our Christian growth and development. It may be through the worries of life; and some of us are more temperamentally prone to worry than others. Worry stands as an opposite to faith, and faith's answer is to turn worries over to God by means of prayer.

A subtle device of Satan – easily fallen into – is his skill at encouraging us to make a bad thing of a good thing. For example, we may discover, with tremendous joy, a new truth about our salvation – perhaps concerning the gifts of the Spirit or the Christian's election. In our enthusiasm we may so stress the value of this new understanding that we neglect what we've already understood, and get things out of balance and go to extremes. Satan loves that! Beware of sudden enthusiasms and aim always at balance.

Satan knows how to get at us when we're down in some way. An obvious example is physical illness or weakness. Paul tells how he had 'a thorn in his flesh' (2 Cor. 12:7). We may be grateful that he doesn't explain what it was, otherwise we might feel that our particular weakness was either greater or smaller than his! Paul just longed to be rid of this physical weakness. He felt he could have served the Lord so much better without it. But the greater problem was that this 'thorn' became 'a messenger of Satan' to torment him (2 Cor. 12:7). Presumably Satan tried to sow doubts in Paul's mind about God's love and purpose, and perhaps argued something like this, 'Do you really believe God hears when you pray about personal things like your "thorn"? Is God able to hear you?' Or maybe Satan suggested that some sin in Paul's life meant that God ignored his prayers. Paul's right response was to keep on praying until he discerned God's will – which, in this case, was that he should accept his weakness and trust the Lord Jesus for His strength in it. Satan, the tempter, will throw temptations at us in any way he can.

How to fight temptation and win

Since the battle so often revolves around temptation, to know how to cope with it and win is essential. There's no slick answer, but the solution involves doing a number of things. The first requirement is *honesty*. We must be honest with ourselves, asking, 'What are my principal temptations? How far do I bring them upon myself?' Temptation itself isn't sin, but it is sinful to place ourselves needlessly before temptation. If a boy's told not to go swimming, he doesn't help himself by taking his swimming trunks with him in case he's tempted! Honesty will lead us to flee from perilous situations (2 Tim. 2:22) and to avoid others where possible. There are many areas in which we can help ourselves, and God requires that we should. Our own attitude is an indispensable key to obtaining victory. If we visit a harbour we may sometimes see yachts setting sail. The interesting feature is that they may be going in opposite directions, although it's the same wind driving them. What makes the difference is the set of their sails. If we would overcome temptation we must honestly 'set our sails' accordingly.

The second requirement is *knowledge*. There are truths we must understand. It's never God who throws temptation at us. It's never right when tempted to say, therefore, 'God is tempting me' (James 1:13). Rather we're to know that God is utterly dependable at all times, and He won't allow us to be tested beyond what we're able to endure. He'll either remove the temptation or increase our strength to cope with it. There's always a God-given way of escape in times of temptation (1 Cor. 10:13).

A third requirement, linked with both honesty and knowledge, is *readiness for drastic action*. The Lord Jesus used dramatic language: 'If your hand causes you to sin, cut it off ...' He went on to say the same thing about the foot and the eye (Mark 9:43-45). Now it's clear that He wasn't suggesting literal amputation, but He was saying something extremely practical and relevant regarding some of our temptations. If we find situations too tough to handle, the answer may not be 'medical' but 'surgical'. If you find that a relationship with someone of the opposite sex always leads you in the wrong direction, then the answer may well be to break off that relationship – tough though that solution may be. That's spiritual 'surgery'. If we find that reading the books of a certain author – good though the story content may be – stirs up unhelpful desires because of the sex element he regularly introduces – the best thing to determine is, 'I'll not read any more of his books.' We can apply this principle to many other temptations.

A fourth requirement is *the exercise of faith*. Deliberately look to God for strength, for the mercy and grace you need as temptations arise (Heb. 4:16). Look for God's way of escape. It may be a promise His Spirit brings to your mind, or a glimpse of the Lord Jesus given to your soul, or some circumstance that shows you that God is there with you. And don't forget to look for spiritual growth in your character as a result of testing, for God doesn't intend that our trials and temptations should be without profit, much as Satan may have intended them for our downfall (James 1:4).

Perhaps a fifth requirement should be added – that of *watchfulness*. Temptations seldom come singly, and they certainly don't stop coming. After one spiritual conflict we may tend to be off our guard and not ready for the next. We may forget that Satan always watches for our moments of unwatchfulness. The Old Testament records the case of Elijah who fought a tremendous battle against the forces of evil in God's Name. He wonderfully overcame, only to succumb quickly afterwards to a fierce bout of depression through his undoubted tiredness after the first battle (1 Kings 18, 19). Watchfulness requires discipline.

DISCIPLINE

Discipline isn't a particularly attractive concept to most of us. Our temperaments and dispositions inevitably vary, and discipline comes more readily to some than to others. Nevertheless, it remains a necessity for all. In writing to Timothy, to encourage him to endure hardship as a Christian, Paul employs three pictures of a Christian – a soldier, an athlete and a farmer (2 Tim. 2:3-6). For a soldier, the first things he meets with upon enlistment are experiences of learning discipline, so that he responds positively to all difficulties and challenges. An athlete disciplines himself to get up early, to eat carefully and to keep his body under control with a view to the competitive event he has in prospect. A farmer works in all weathers and disciplines himself to seize opportunities for sowing and harvesting his crops, while others may relax and laze. The Christian is to be like all three!

Aim to be disciplined in your use of time. The amount of time we can give to prayer and Bible study – both essentials for the successful fighting of the battle – hinge much upon the time we go to bed and the time we get up in the morning. Work out the number of hours of sleep you require and consistently aim at that. Relaxation too is necessary for productive work and a healthy mind. Determine, therefore, what your best forms of recreation are and how long you should devote to them each week.

When we are properly disciplined, we're not simply carried along by the events of life, but we steer them in the right direction and make the best use of the time. A disciplined Christian is a difficult target for the enemy of our souls.

Caution!

I feel I must mention a few snares to avoid regarding this battle we've been trying to describe and understand. The first snare is of going to extremes with regard to it. One extreme is to ignore totally the reality of this battle so that we're completely unprepared for it. The opposite extreme is to exaggerate the battle, so that we spend a lot of our time thinking about our enemy. The battle is real, and not imaginary, but it's not to be the principal way in which we think of the Christian life. To return to Paul's pictures, we are not only soldiers, but we're also like athletes and farmers – we've exciting goals before us, by means of which we may discover tremendous personal fulfilment.

Another snare is to lose our joy in the Christian life. The battle against the world, the flesh and the devil often highlights our weaknesses and sins. Sometimes we'll become incredibly fed up with ourselves because of our persistent sinfulness. We will completely identify with Paul who described himself as the worst of sinners (1 Tim. 1:15). But we're not meant to lose our joy in the Christian life on account of the battle. If we do, then two things at least have happened. First, we've forgotten that it's a *good* fight of faith. Remember, as we said earlier, we wouldn't know anything of the fight's reality and of such bitter disappointment with ourselves, if we hadn't in fact been born again into God's family and His Son's kingdom. And, secondly, to have lost our joy we must have taken our eyes off our Lord Jesus Christ – the mistake Satan wants us to fall into more than any other. Our Lord's death for us dealt finally and completely with all our sins – past, present and future. As we honestly confess them, God assures us of His complete forgiveness and cleansing.

As we fix our eyes on the Lord Jesus, we remember too the glorious truth of our union with Him and that we are meant to live the Christian life not in our own strength but by His power. The One who is in us 'is greater than the one who is in the world' (1 John 4:4). With our eyes on the Lord Jesus and His strength, we're ready for Satan and all his attacks. We can identify with David who declared, 'Praise be to the Lord, my Rock, who trains my hands for war, my fingers for battle. He is my loving God and my fortress, my stronghold and my deliverer, my shield, in whom I take refuge ...' (Ps. 144:1, 2).

A Prayer

Thank You, Father, for rescuing me from the dominion of darkness and bringing me into Your Son's glorious kingdom. I praise and thank You that it's the *good* fight of faith that I'm to fight. In times of temptation please turn my eyes to the Lord Jesus, so that I may call upon Him for His power and strength to overcome. Where I need to be more disciplined, please give me the courage and honesty to take appropriate action. Thank

You that You always want me to triumph through the Lord Jesus and to know the joy of Your salvation. I pray in Jesus' Name, Amen.

QUESTIONS

1. What would you identify as the principal ways in which you become aware of Satan's attacks and activity?
2. In what areas of life do you find discipline most difficult? What positive steps can you take to help yourself in these areas?

BIBLE REFERENCES FOR FURTHER STUDY

THE BATTLE
John 16:33; Ephesians 6:12; 1 Timothy 6:12; 2 Timothy 4:7; 1 Peter 5:9; Revelation 6:11.

THE ENEMY
Luke 22:31; John 8:44; 2 Corinthians 4:4; Ephesians 4:27; 6:11, 12, 16; 1 Peter 5:8; 1 John 3:8; 5:19.

THE ARMOUR
Romans 13:12; 2 Corinthians 10:4; Ephesians 6:11, 13-17; 1 Thessalonians 5:8.

THE WEAPONS
2 Corinthians 6:7; 10:3-5; Ephesians 6:17, 18; Hebrews 4:12, 16.

TEMPTATION
1 Corinthians 7:5; 10:12, 13; Galatians 6:1; 1 Thessalonians 3:5; Hebrews 2:18; 4:14-16; James 1:13-15; 4:7; 1 Peter 5:8, 9.

5

Make Jesus Lord!

The Lord Jesus never allowed people to follow Him without their first considering the cost. He didn't call anyone to discipleship under false pretences. He made potential disciples read 'the small print' so that they wouldn't have any unhappy surprises. 'Count the cost' was His frequent theme. The principle remains true. He wants us to follow Him, understanding from the beginning what's required, and He wants us to continue following Him to the end of our lives. Compromise and letting Him down should be out of the question.

'JESUS IS LORD!'

When we say 'Jesus is Lord!' we declare a number of important truths about Him. These truths were more obvious in the first century when that public confession was originally made, but they need to be grasped by us too.

The title 'Lord' is the Old Testament equivalent of the name of God – 'Jehovah'. The first Christians were Jews who knew that there is only one God. They understood what they were doing, therefore, when they called Jesus 'Lord'. They were proclaiming

Him to be the divine Lord, the One who has the highest place and is worthy of our worship, service and obedience. To call Jesus 'Lord' is to declare Him to be God. The Bible explains that Jesus Christ is God the Son, the Second Person of the Trinity, who is one with the Father and the Holy Spirit.

The confession that 'Jesus is Lord!' brought trouble for many early Christians since 'Lord' was also the title frequently given to the Roman emperors when they chose to regard themselves as gods rather than men. Roman citizens were then called upon to burn incense to Caesar and declare 'Caesar is Lord!' But no Christian could do that. Rather he would have to affirm, 'Caesar isn't Lord, but Jesus is!'

An outstanding example was Polycarp, Bishop of Smyrna, who was martyred for his faith in the Lord Jesus in 155, at the age of 86. Many tried to persuade Polycarp to give in to the demands of the Roman authorities. 'What harm is there,' they asked, 'in saying "Lord Caesar", and in offering incense, and so on, and thus saving yourself?' At first he didn't answer them, but since they persisted, he said, 'I don't intend to do what you advise.' Eventually he was led before the Roman Proconsul, who also tried to persuade him. 'Have respect to your age,' he said. 'Swear by Caesar and I will release you; curse the Christ.' To which Polycarp answered, 'Eighty and six years have I served Him, and He has done me no wrong; how then can I blaspheme my King who saved me?' And so he was burned alive. He wasn't the first Christian martyr, and many have followed, and no doubt will continue to do so. To call Jesus 'Lord' may not be as costly for us, but we should be as ready to make that profession when it's hard as when it's easy.

In addition, the title 'Lord' was the word used in the first century for a master in relation to his slaves. The ancient world depended upon slavery, and many of the first Gentile Christians

were slaves. To a slave his master's word was law: whatever his
master said had to be obeyed. A slave had often become his master's possession through purchase in a slave-market; a price had
been paid for him, and his master looked for some return. The
Christian's Master – our Lord Jesus Christ – has set us free from
the spiritual bondage we were under through sin and Satan's
dominion, and He has done so at tremendous cost – His own
blood. We delight to call Him 'Master' and to declare ourselves
His 'slaves' or 'servants' even though He chooses to call us His
friends.

The earliest Christian statement of belief was contained in
the three words: 'Jesus is Lord!' Christians made this confession
at their baptism and upon their admission to the church of Jesus
Christ. As we've seen, it would in some cases bring them into
immediate conflict with the society of which they were part.

It's unfortunate that throughout the centuries baptism
has been allowed to divide Christians because of differing
views concerning it, especially as to whether or not it should
be administered to young infants or only to adult believers.
We'll try not to get involved in that controversy insofar as we
can say, without argument – hopefully – that every Christian
ought to be baptised since the Lord Jesus Christ commands it.
Every Christian, looking back upon baptism, sees it as a symbol
of repentance, faith in the Lord Jesus and the desire to live
a new life through the power of the Holy Spirit. Baptism also
symbolises the Christian's entry into all the benefits of the Lord
Jesus Christ's death and resurrection: all that He accomplished
on the cross and by His rising again is ours.

It's particularly interesting to note that baptism is 'into the
name of Jesus' (Acts 8:16; 19:5), since the expression 'into the
name' of someone was used commercially for the transfer of
property. If I sell my car, it's no longer in my name but in the

name of its new owner – and all the rights over it are his and not mine. Our baptism declares the Lord Jesus Christ's rightful ownership of our lives – He both created us and 'bought us back' – and we rightly call Him 'Lord'.

DISCIPLESHIP

The profession in baptism we made of Jesus as 'Lord' then needs to be worked out in daily practice. The Lordship of Jesus means His rule of our life. That isn't something to be afraid of, since He's the very best Lord or Master we could have. Nevertheless, He should reign in our life. I wonder if you noticed in Polycarp's testimony how he referred to the Lord Jesus as his 'King'? Christian language – especially as it's found in hymns and songs – speaks often of the Lord Jesus as Lord, Master, Teacher, King – and they add up to the same idea.

The Lord Jesus Christ Himself must be our guide as to how we are to understand His Lordship over our life. The picture He used most was that of discipleship. Discipleship seems perhaps an old-fashioned word, but there's no real contemporary replacement. A disciple is basically a follower and a learner. The word has obvious links with the word 'discipline', and a disciple is someone under the discipline of another as, for example, a learner-driver is under the discipline of his instructor. Christians are to be under Jesus' discipline and instruction.

The experience of the first Christians – or disciples – helps us. 'As Jesus walked beside the Sea of Galilee, he saw Simon and his brother Andrew casting a net into the lake, for they were fishermen. "Come, follow me," Jesus said, "and I will make you fishers of men." At once they left their nets and followed him' (Mark 1:16-18). 'Come, follow ...' that was the first instruction. He told them what He would make them – 'fishers of men' – and they then came under His direct instruction for three years.

Calling Jesus 'Lord' means following Him and looking to Him for instruction as we would to no one else.

NO EASY WAY

To be in such close fellowship with the Lord Jesus was a tremendous privilege for those first disciples, but it was also challenging and uncomfortable as He spelt out to them what following Him means in practice: 'If anyone would come after me, he must deny himself and take up his cross and follow me. For whoever wants to save his life will lose it, but whoever loses his life for me and for the gospel will save it' (Mark 8:34, 35).

Calling Jesus 'Lord' – or, using this other way of putting things, discipleship – means denying ourselves. This isn't something superficial like going without sugar in our tea or coffee, or doing without sweets in Lent! It's something deep and profound – in fact, life-transforming. It's to say 'No' to self when self's demands contradict God's. It's to say 'Yes' to God's will when our natural desires would lead us in a contrary direction. This has obvious relevance to our physical and sexual desires. To call Jesus 'Lord' is to say 'Yes' to what He says about purity and to say 'No' to what our body may tell us is natural or acceptable to society. It also has specific relevance to our choices in life. To call Jesus 'Lord' is to say 'Yes' to the path of duty and 'No' to what may be much more comfortable and undisturbing.

Linked with denying ourselves is taking up our cross. Here again we mustn't debase this concept by thinking of it simply in terms of some passing chore or perhaps putting up with a difficult relative. It goes much deeper than that. The Lord Jesus certainly isn't suggesting that we can share in the redemptive work of the cross. His cross is absolutely unique in what He accomplished by it for our salvation. We need to be clear, therefore, as to what the Lord Jesus has in view by His use of this picture.

Two things seem plain. First, when people saw a man carrying a cross through their town or village, they knew that it was a one-way journey; he wouldn't be seen going that way again. Secondly, the cross summed up God's will for the Lord Jesus. In the Garden of Gethsemane His natural inclination, as He anticipated the sufferings of the cross, was to pray, 'Take this cup of suffering from Me'. But, denying Himself – saying 'No' to Himself – He prayed, 'Yet not what I will, but what You will'. To take up our cross is to be totally committed to God's will, as the Lord Jesus was, wherever that commitment may take us, with no turning back.

Now that's extremely practical and down-to-earth. We may, for example, be quite happy to follow God's will until perhaps there's a conflict over what we want and what we know God wants. When we've genuinely taken up the cross, the issue isn't in dispute – we'll go God's way whatever the cost, even if it means breaking off a relationship, changing the direction of our career or anything else.

THE INDISPUTABLE EXAMPLE

Making Jesus Lord means uncompromising commitment to His example. He expressed this principle many times, and nowhere more clearly than when He washed the disciples' feet. ' "Do you understand what I have done for you?" he asked them. "You call me 'Teacher' and 'Lord', and rightly so, for that is what I am . Now that I, your Lord and Teacher, have washed your feet, you also should wash one another's feet. I have set you an example that you should do as I have done for you"' (John 13:12-15).

Let's explore what we mean in practice by following Jesus' example. It must obviously include standing up for all that He represents – and in particular truth and righteousness. The Lord Jesus declared Himself to be 'the Truth', and He is described as 'the Righteous One' (1 John 2:1). Christians who call Jesus 'Lord' must be committed, therefore, to truth. That's more demanding than we may think at first. We must first be committed to seeking after truth on a daily basis. That's made straightforward through God's provision of the Scriptures, the Bible, and the gift of the divine Interpreter, God the Holy Spirit. But we need to give time to our pursuit of the truth – whether by our own reading of the Bible or our listening to instruction from it. But to read and to hear aren't sufficient: we must respond to the truth. Obedience to the Scriptures needs to be as constant and regular as breathing is to our body. A proper response to the Scriptures requires openness since we'll find ourselves directed, rebuked and called to action by them. We'll learn to face up to truth when it's uncomfortable and to be honest before God, and then with others.

Christians who call Jesus 'Lord' must also be committed to righteousness – not a word we use much in contemporary speech. The essence of righteousness is 'doing the right thing'. The apostle Peter explains that one of the major purposes of our Lord's atoning death was our commitment to righteousness: 'He himself bore our sins in his body on the tree, so that we might die to sins and live for righteousness' (1 Pet. 2:24). Before we were Christians we weren't totally ignorant of righteousness, but instead of automatically asking, 'What's the right thing to do?' we were more inclined to ask, 'What's the convenient or easiest thing to do?'

Truthfulness and righteousness go hand in hand insofar as I can only know what the right thing to do is if I'm first prepared to ask, 'What is true?' Let me illustrate: suppose someone says, 'Please spend some time with me', now what should I do? To know what is right, I must first ask what is true. Who is it who says, 'Please spend some time with me'? If the truth is that it's my wife, then the right thing to do is to respond gladly. But if the person who says it is a woman other than my wife, then the right response is to refuse. I've chosen a straightforward illustration in order to make the point. Ask, 'What's the truth?' and then usually we'll know what's right. The Lord Jesus Christ is the Light of the world, and when we walk with Him we don't walk in the shadows – we don't countenance either thoughts or actions that are doubtful, and we don't engage in the kind of things people prefer to do in the dark or when no one is looking. By calling Jesus 'Lord' we aim to do what pleases Him in every area of life.

A CONTINUAL PROCESS

All this seems a tall order! And probably we find ourselves conscious of many failures in our acknow-ledgement of Jesus' Lordship. There's a difference between our genuinely calling Jesus 'Lord' and our actually achieving it in practice in *every* area of life. But it's genuineness of intention that our Lord Jesus looks for first.

I've found it helpful to think of my life like a house. As you step through its front door, you enter a hall, from which there lead off the various rooms of the house. Now when we wish people to visit us, we invite them in, and we perhaps then take them into only one or two of the rooms. If they were to stay, of course, they would know the house better. Becoming a Christian is like inviting the Lord Jesus Christ into the house of our life. We may genuinely invite Him in and want Him to share our life, but we may not immediately think of opening up every room to Him – the rooms marked, for example, time and leisure, money, friendships, career and ambition. But as we know Him better, we should appreciate that every room should not only be opened to Him, but made acceptable to Him. Let's look at the areas of life we've mentioned.

The Lord Jesus should be Lord of our time. Now that doesn't mean that we will have no time for relaxation and leisure – far from it! He's the perfect Master, and He knows – better than we do – our minds' and bodies' requirement of relaxation. But the difference now that we're Christians is that we want to honour God in our use of time. Time is perhaps the most valuable commodity we possess. As Christians we'll not want to 'kill' time, but to put it to good account. Some of us may need to discipline ourselves to make time for relaxation, and others of us that we don't give it too much time! When Jesus is 'Lord', there's a balance about our lives and how we spend our time.

The Lord Jesus should be Lord of our money and our material possessions. A practical outworking of this is tithing – the giving of a tenth of our income to God. It's nowhere laid down in the New Testament that it should be a tenth, but that was the Old Testament pattern for God's people, and most Christians find it a helpful guide. What proportion of our income we give remains a personal matter to determine, but what is plain is that our giving should be regular, cheerful and in proportion to our income (1 Cor. 16:2; 2 Cor. 9:7). But the Lordship of the Lord Jesus over our money and possessions doesn't end there. We must recognise that all we possess belongs to Him. We may use our home, our car and, in fact, our every asset, in the interests of His kingdom.

The Lord Jesus should be Lord of our friendships, and not least the kind of friendship that may lead to marriage. Inevitably we make new friends when we become Christians and, for the most part, they will be Christian friends. But it's important not to cut ourselves off either from our former non-Christian friends or from the people whom we get to know in the course of our daily work or leisure pursuits. It happens sometimes that they may cut themselves off from us because we don't go along with them in activities which we no longer enjoy – obvious examples are loose-living, drinking and gambling.

If ever a particular friendship seems likely to compromise our loyalty with the Lord Jesus or to dampen our zeal to follow Him, then we'll be wise to control it carefully or even to break it off. This must especially be the course of action if it's a relationship with someone of the opposite sex, a relationship which could lead to marriage.

The Bible's quite plain that a Christian should only marry another Christian and not marry an unbeliever. When a person becomes a Christian, and his or her partner is not yet a Christian, that's another matter: the duty of the Christian partner then is to win over the partner for the Lord Jesus Christ (1 Pet. 3:1).

The Bible teaches that we may marry anyone we wish, but he or she must belong to the Lord (1 Cor. 7:39; cf. 2 Cor. 6:14, 15): it makes sense. The love of a husband and wife is a very special love and an all-demanding love. If they both love Jesus Christ, then they'll be thrilled to devote their lives to Him together. But if they don't both love Him, then one partner's love for Him is likely to become a divisive factor.

A basic requirement for a happy marriage is the ability of two people to share totally in each other's interests. For a Christian to marry someone who isn't a Christian can be a recipe for disaster because the marriage begins with a vital area where there isn't a genuine sharing.

This principle doesn't at once rule out friendship with someone of the opposite sex who isn't a Christian. In fact, such a friendship may be a God-given opportunity to point the friend to faith in the Lord Jesus. But the principle does mean being clear from the beginning that a friendship can be only a friendship while the situation remains. If it's found too difficult to handle, then the best course of action is to bring the relationship to an end before the other person is hurt too much. I've observed that it's always an encouraging sign if an unconverted friend is willing to come to church regularly with a Christian, and this has more often than not led to conversion. To stop before it's too late in a relationship is so important; otherwise the heart tends to rule the mind, and what we want takes precedence over what we know to be right.

It would be sad, however, if we have a negative view of friendships, because the delightful truth is that if our lives are genuinely under the Lordship of Christ, His plans for us — whether to marry or to remain single — are perfect. If it's to be marriage, then He will bring the right partner across our path as we give Him His rightful place in our affections.

The Lord Jesus should be Lord of our career and ambitions. Christian service isn't simply service performed by those who are described as 'full-time' in it. All that we do may be of service for Jesus Christ as we do it with His praise in view and as His servants rather than simply as the employees of human employers. His will extends to our daily work and the progress we should make in it.

Being a Christian at work doesn't mean that we shouldn't be ambitious. The Lord Jesus may well choose to plant specific ambitions in our mind. Our motivation, however, will never be just personal prestige or a better salary, but honouring Jesus Christ by the way we do our work. Promotion will never be because we've ingratiated ourselves with people, but on the grounds of consistent hard work done with the Lord Jesus' honour in view. If we are promoted, we won't allow compromise to spoil our witness — loyalty to the Lord Jesus and integrity will be at the top of our list, no matter how difficult maintaining them may sometimes be in the hard cut and thrust of working life.

GUIDANCE

In all of these areas we've mentioned, we'll regularly be wanting to discover God's will. To make Jesus Lord means looking to Him for guidance, as we look to no one else. It's worth stressing that our actually making Jesus Lord in our life is the best possible guarantee of discovering God's will because it fulfils the condition God lays down for His guidance in the Book of Proverbs: 'In all your ways acknowledge him, and he will make your paths straight' (Prov. 3:6).

Those words underline God's principal form of guidance: He makes our paths straight. That's another way of saying that we see the way forward. God seldom gives guidance before we require it, and when it comes it usually shows us only the next step. If we saw too far ahead, we might trust in ourselves too much and make mistakes.

Guidance is the particular province of the Holy Spirit, and He uses various means to direct us into God's will. Since so much is at stake if we go in the wrong direction, we'll find that He guides us usually by a number of factors coming together – not necessarily all of them at once, but usually more than just one.

Let's imagine that we have to make a decision about our job – perhaps whether to stay where we are or to consider moving. First, we should see what guidance our circumstances provide. Presumably there will be things which have happened which have made us feel we should review our situation. We should ask God for wisdom to know how far we should be influenced by these occurrences and at the same time check our motives for thinking of a move.

Secondly, we'll probably find an inner conviction developing as to the best and right course of action. We shouldn't despise this, especially if when we share this conviction with God in prayer a sense of peace follows. One of the ways He assures us of His will is by the gift of His peace (Col. 3:15). A third factor often is the conviction of others, especially Christian friends who pray for us and who are able to look at our situation in a more detached way.

The most important factor, however, is the gift of discernment (Phil. 1:9-11). As we continually surrender ourselves to God, in the light of His mercy to us in the Lord Jesus, He renews our minds so that we are able to test and approve what God's will is (Rom. 12:2). This ability to discern God's will grows as we know and increasingly obey the Scriptures – especially on a daily basis. Through the growing spiritual understanding of God this gives, the Holy Spirit enables us to weigh up our circumstances, matched often by the convictions of other Christians whose counsel we seek. When Jesus' Lordship is real in our life we are happy only when we 'stand firm in all the will of God, mature and fully assured' (Col. 4:12).

CHRIST AND HIS CHURCH

Jesus' Lordship in our lives can't be separated from a strong relationship to His people and faithfulness to them. As we've mentioned before, the question is sometimes asked, 'Can't you be a Christian without going to church?' The answer has to be 'Yes'. But the truth is that we'll never find a healthy Christian who doesn't long to be in fellowship with other Christians. The most important reason for this is the Bible's revelation that the church is actually the body of which the Lord Jesus Christ is the Head. It's worthwhile pausing to ponder this truth. Whatever we do to the church, we do to the Lord Jesus Christ. When the risen Lord Jesus met Saul on the road to Damascus, He didn't say to him, 'Saul, Saul, why do you persecute *Christians*?' but rather 'Saul, Saul, why do you persecute *me*?' (Acts 9:4).

Loving Jesus Christ and loving His church are two sides of the same coin. Similarly, serving His church and serving Him are one and the same. In the account our Lord Jesus gave of the Last Judgment, He illustrated how He, as the Chief Shepherd, will separate the sheep from the goats – true believers from those who are not (Matt. 25:31-46). True believers will have proved their love for Christ's people, and He will reward them, saying, 'Whatever you did for one of the least of these brothers of mine, you did for me' (Matt. 25:40). We may test the reality of Jesus' Lordship in our lives by our love for His people and our sense of commitment to them. 'A new command I give you,' Jesus says, 'Love one another. As I have loved you, so you must love one another. By this all men will know that you are my disciples, if you love one another' (John 13:34, 35).

CLUES TO SUCCESS

When we begin the Christian life, we call Jesus 'Lord' for the first time; but that's only the beginning! Changing circumstances of life – marriage, new spheres of employment, fresh responsibilities and simply growing older – all demand a reassessment of what Jesus' Lordship means in practice. Loving the Lord Jesus, we'll naturally want to succeed in maintaining His practical Lordship in our lives, and two clues to success are worth sharing. First, we need to maintain clear views of our Saviour. It's so easy to get sidetracked from the centrality of our Lord Jesus – whether by sheer busy-ness or by preoccupation with secondary matters. The Christian life is all about knowing Jesus Christ. He's the centre of all God's purposes, and through Him we know the Father. The focus of our Bible reading and study needs to be on knowing Him. As we know Him, we'll find no difficulty in wanting to make Him Lord in all our changing circumstances.

The second clue is the maintenance of our daily obedience to the Scriptures, either as we read them or hear them taught and preached. There won't be a day when God doesn't call us to obedience, and if we make sure that we're open to His voice and responsive to it, our lives will display the attractiveness of Jesus' Lordship. It's worthwhile making it our daily habit to ask, 'Lord, what do you want me to do?'

A Prayer

Father, I realise that it's a miracle of Your grace that my eyes have been opened to see the light of the knowledge of Your glory in the face of Your Son Jesus Christ; and that it's only through the working of Your Holy Spirit in my life that I can call Jesus 'Lord' and mean it. Thank You for Your graciousness to me and for the gift of Your Spirit.

Here and now I want to make Jesus Lord of every area of my life – my time, my possessions, my money, my friendships, my career and my ambitions. Please give me a tender conscience about anything that might compromise a sincere devotion to the Lord Jesus and His total ownership of my life. Give me the honesty to admit where I'm compromising and the strength to renew my wholehearted commitment to Him. Show me more and more of His glory so that my first motive may be love for Him. I ask this for His Name's sake. Amen.

Questions

1. How would you explain to others what the Lordship of Jesus Christ means in your life?
2. We've considered the Lordship of our Lord Jesus Christ in relation to our time, money and possessions, friendships, career and ambitions; are there other areas where we are aware that His Lordship needs to be established and maintained?

BIBLE REFERENCES FOR FURTHER STUDY

EXAMPLES OF OLD TESTAMENT PASSAGES SPEAKING OF THE LORD JEHOVAH BEING APPLIED TO CHRIST IN THE NEW TESTAMENT

Numbers 21:5, 6, cf. 1 Corinthians 10:9; Psalm 102:25-27 cf. Hebrews 1:10; Isaiah 6:1-10, cf. John 12:40, 41; Isaiah 8:13, 14, cf. Luke 2:34, Romans 9:3; Isaiah 40:3, 4, cf. John 1:23; Isaiah 45:22, 23, cf. Romans 14:11, Philippians 2:10, 11; Malachi 3:1, cf. Matthew 11:10.

JESUS' TEACHING ABOUT DISCIPLESHIP

Matthew 10:37-39; 12:48-50; 16:24, 25; Luke 9:62; 14:25-35; 16:13; John 12:23-26; 13:35; 14:21, 24.

GUIDANCE

Psalm 23:3; 25:12; 48:14; 73:24; 119:24; Proverbs 3:6; Isaiah 30:21; Romans 12:1, 2; Philippians 1:9-11.

THE IMPOSSIBILITY OF SEPARATING LOVE FOR JESUS CHRIST FROM LOVE FOR HIS PEOPLE, HIS CHURCH

Matthew 25:31-46; John 13:34, 35; 15:10-12, 17; 1 John 3:14-18; 4:7-12, 19-21.

6

Share your faith!

The good news of our Lord Jesus is too good to keep to ourselves! If we look back to our conversion, we'll probably recall how someone – or perhaps several people – shared their faith in the Lord Jesus Christ with us. It's now our privilege to pass the good news on to others.

Nothing surpasses personal recommendation, and there's nothing more important than our commending the Lord Jesus to people who don't yet know Him. We may not feel that we can express ourselves well at first, but that shouldn't stop us. Reality shines through even when words are stumbling and faltering. As people listen to us they are able to discern whether or not what we say has the ring of truth. Better a clumsy telling of others about the Lord Jesus with the ring of reality than an eloquent statement of faith without it.

A man born blind was healed by the Lord Jesus. Those who questioned him tried to cast doubt upon his experience of Jesus' healing power. His answer, though simple, was sufficient to confound them: 'One thing I do know,' he said, 'I was blind but now I see!' (John 9:25).

It's impossible to be a healthy Christian without feeling an obligation and inner compulsion to share our faith. The early apostles were forbidden to talk about Jesus, but they replied, 'We cannot help speaking about what we have seen and heard' (Acts 4:20). 'Christ's love compels us' (2 Cor. 5:14) – our love for Him and the love He puts in our hearts for others. We owe so much to the Lord Jesus. Since He died for us, the least we can do is to live to make Him known and to share with others the great purpose of His death. The need others have of salvation is as great as ours. What's more, the change that has taken place in our life – and which continues – is bound to prompt questions. Where then do we begin?

KNOW WHAT YOU BELIEVE!

Faith began for all of us when God gave us an understanding through His Word – whether read or preached – of specific truths about Himself, His Son and our need of the salvation the Lord Jesus died and rose again to make possible (see, for example, 1 Cor. 15:1-8). God's Spirit gave us time to take them in, and He helped us understand them by His unique illumination.

But those primary truths are only the foundation or the beginning. There's much more truth about God and His purposes to understand – what the apostle Paul called 'the whole will of God' (Acts 20:27). We know too that there's a difference between understanding something ourselves and our ability to communicate it to others. We need to know a subject especially well if we're to share it and answer people's questions. So we must not only know what we believe, but we must know the facts of the Christian faith well enough to pass them on.

The apostles saw the importance of this, and they taught that there are certain truths – a body of teaching which we call 'doctrines' – which they had to pass on to all believers if their apostolic task was to be done properly (1 Cor. 15:1, 3; 1 Thess. 4:1, 2). Paul reminded the Romans, for example, of 'the form of teaching to which you were entrusted' (Rom. 6:17). 'The faith' is a frequent New Testament expression to describe these basic foundation truths that all Christians believe. Jude urged his readers to 'contend for the faith that was once for all entrusted to the saints' (Jude 3).

It's easy to see, therefore, why early on in its history the church recognised the importance of creeds. (Creed comes from the Latin word 'credo', meaning 'I believe'). Most churches have what is described as a doctrinal basis – in other words, a statement of belief. A creed provides a programme for study and a means of being sure about the most important aspects of our faith.

THE APOSTLES' CREED

A good starting point is the Apostles' Creed. We can trace back its beginnings to the middle of the second century. It's a brief yet comprehensive statement of basic Christian belief:

> I believe in God the Father Almighty, Maker of heaven and earth; and in Jesus Christ His only Son our Lord, who was conceived by the Holy Spirit, born of the virgin Mary, suffered under Pontius Pilate, was crucified, dead and buried, He descended into hell; the third day He rose again from the dead, He ascended into Heaven, and sits on the right hand of God the Father the Almighty; from thence He shall come to judge the living and the dead. I believe in the Holy Spirit; the holy catholic Church; the communion of saints; the forgiveness of sins; the resurrection of the body, and the life everlasting.

The Apostles' Creed provides a concise agenda for studying the faith we profess. Let us survey it briefly so as to indicate the areas of study it opens up. (At the conclusion of this chapter you'll find a list of Bible references which will enable you to study the subjects in greater depth and to answer some of the questions we are going to ask.)

I BELIEVE

How does the Bible define faith? And how does it say faith comes about?

IN GOD

What is God like? What are the evidences of God's existence? How does God make Himself known to us so that we are able to trust Him?

THE FATHER ALMIGHTY, MAKER OF HEAVEN AND EARTH

Is God everyone's Father? Or is He only the Father of those who believe in His Son? In what ways is God's power shown? If God is all-powerful, how do we explain the dreadful things that happen in the world? How did God create everything? What was His purpose? What spoilt it?

AND IN JESUS CHRIST HIS ONLY SON OUR LORD

What does the name 'Jesus' mean? Do the two titles 'Christ' and 'Lord' have significance? Why is the Lord Jesus Christ called 'the Son of God'? In what ways is His Sonship different from ours when we become Christians?

WHO WAS CONCEIVED BY THE HOLY SPIRIT, BORN OF THE VIRGIN MARY

Why was His virgin conception necessary? Is it a vital truth?

SUFFERED UNDER PONTIUS PILATE

Is Pilate an historical character? What was Pilate's verdict about Jesus?

WAS CRUCIFIED, DEAD AND BURIED

Why did Jesus die? What evidences were there that He was dead? How certain is it that the exact place of His burial was known?

HE DESCENDED INTO HELL

Is hell as real a place as heaven? What is the difference between Hades and Gehenna? Why did Jesus have to descend into Hades?

THE THIRD DAY HE ROSE AGAIN FROM THE DEAD

What are the evidences for Jesus' resurrection? Why did He rise? What significance does His resurrection have for us now?

HE ASCENDED INTO HEAVEN, AND SITS ON THE RIGHT HAND OF GOD THE FATHER ALMIGHTY

What is heaven? What is the importance of Jesus' ascension? What does His sitting on the right hand of God signify?

FROM THENCE HE SHALL COME TO JUDGE THE LIVING AND THE DEAD

How and when will Jesus come back? What will happen at the judgment?

I BELIEVE IN THE HOLY SPIRIT

Who is the Holy Spirit? Is He a Person? What do we mean by 'the Trinity'? What is the Holy Spirit's work?

THE HOLY CATHOLIC CHURCH

What is meant by the word 'catholic'? What is the Church? Who belongs to the Church? What are God's plans for the Church? What should our relationship be to the church in its local context?

THE COMMUNION OF SAINTS

Who are the 'saints'? Are Christians really one – that is to say, united? What has happened to those Christians who have died?

THE FORGIVENESS OF SINS

Do all need forgiveness? How may it be obtained? How complete is it? What should Christians do when they sin?

THE RESURRECTION OF THE BODY

Is everyone to be raised from the dead? What will the resurrection of the dead mean for the Christian? What will the resurrection body be like?

AND THE LIFE EVERLASTING

What do we mean by everlasting life? What's the opposite of everlasting life?

These questions are all basic and important; and we shouldn't allow ourselves to be satisfied until we know the answers and are able to communicate them effectively. We need to grasp these truths inside out, knowing where they are taught in the Bible, and how to prove and illustrate them. It's an exciting lifetime's task! The excitement springs from the fact that the more we understand these truths the more wonderful we discover them to be. And there's no greater excitement than seeing others come to understand them so that they put their faith in Jesus Christ.

There are many books written with a view to helping us share our faith. But always let the Bible be your primary guide, and accept the guidance of the books only as they clearly show you what the Bible teaches. Aim to be moulded in your beliefs by the Bible's teaching rather than by the books. Be prepared for hard work, but its rewards will be tremendous, both for you and for others, and the Holy Spirit delights to be our Teacher.

LIVE WHAT YOU BELIEVE!

As important as knowing what we believe is living out what we believe. People have a right to expect that what we say about our faith in God through His Son Jesus Christ should be demonstrated and proved in our own lives, and this is especially relevant when we are witnessing to our families, friends and colleagues at work.

Opportunities for Christian witness may occur sometimes with complete strangers. We may find ourselves entering into a conversation on a train or bus with someone we've never met before. Perhaps a newspaper headline prompts a discussion about the state of the world. The other person may comment, 'I don't know what the world's coming to! Is there any hope?' As Christians we do have hope for the future, and we ought to share it on such occasions. Situations may arise in our daily work where a customer or client shares a personal anxiety and perhaps asks, 'What would you do?' Your honest answer probably would be, 'Well, I would begin by praying about it ...' We should not hesitate to say so. When we spend time as patients in a hospital ward, we frequently discover ourselves getting close to total strangers and talking about extremely personal issues. These opportunities are to be seized, but always with courtesy and gentleness.

But more often than not, we have to earn the right to share our faith with people whom we know well. This is especially the case at home, with our friends and those with whom we work. As we've thought earlier – in our first chapter – our conversion may produce the reaction, 'Whatever's happened to you?' People may be surprised, interested or even alarmed!

Some will certainly be asking themselves, 'Will it last?' 'How real is it?' Or their reaction may be, 'Let's put this Christianity of his to the test!' And they are right. 'The proof of the pudding is in the eating!' Their watching and testing of us isn't out of place: if we're genuine, we'll be proved genuine. They will watch us more than we know to see if we are really different and if we practise what we preach. They'll probably set much higher standards for us than for themselves. But as we prove by our lives that Jesus Christ is at work in us, we'll earn the right to speak about Him.

The most difficult sphere – and yet the most important – is the home. Once we've told our family what's happened to us – and it would be dishonest not to do so – we'll be wise not to say much until our changed lives have had time to speak. It's particularly difficult for children to share their faith with their parents. Parents instinctively feel that they should know better than their children! A wife may find that her new-found faith could drive a wedge between her and her husband, and she must do her best to see that she's not the one responsible for such a situation. The answer in such tricky domestic situations is to 'win' people (1 Pet. 3:1).

It's possible to win individuals to faith in the Lord Jesus as we share our faith not so much by words but by the way we live. It may take months and even years, but it's often God's way. We are to make sure that our lives 'in every way … make the teaching about God our Saviour attractive' (Titus 2:10). To achieve this, we need to pull our weight at home and take our share of duties like the household chores – and that can be quite a change for some of us! But faith in Jesus Christ brings such a revolution!

We should have a reputation at work for honesty and reliability. We should be easy to work with, the kind of people who make personal relationships run smoothly. Inevitably people will then know that they can trust us, and as they do so God will provide unique situations for sharing the good news of the Lord Jesus – and sometimes the very opportunities for which He's put us in that place of employment. As we live what we believe, the God-given moments for witness will be there!

BE READY TO GIVE AN ANSWER FOR WHAT YOU BELIEVE!

Our order in this chapter is important. First, we must know what we believe. Second, we must live what we believe. Inevitably consistent Christian conduct will provoke questions, and then we must be ready to give answers. That's a clear New Testament instruction: 'Always be prepared to give an answer to everyone who asks you to give the reason for the hope that you have. But do this with gentleness and respect, keeping a clear conscience, so that those who speak maliciously against your good behaviour in Christ may be ashamed of their slander' (1 Pet. 3:15, 16). Note the emphasis upon 'good behaviour in Christ' – that backs up what we've said about earning our right to speak.

It's interesting that Peter mentions people asking us specifically about our 'hope'. The Lord Jesus Christ Himself is our hope – all that we look forward to in the future is bound up in Him and His triumphant return. Part of our hope in Him is our assurance of 'the resurrection of the body and the life everlasting' that we've already mentioned. Peter rightly implies that people should soon come to recognise that Christians are people of hope. Once more this underlines the importance of our conduct since the apostle John tells us that if our hope is in the Lord Jesus and in His coming again, practical holiness will be promoted in our daily life (1 John 3:3). It will sometimes be when sad circumstances like bereavement and serious illness come to us that our non-Christian friends and colleagues will see in our attitudes and reactions how brightly our hope burns.

People do ask questions when they see genuine expressions of Christian faith, and especially when they see it shining through adversity and difficulty. Those questions are key opportunities. When people question us they are much more ready to listen than if we tried to make the running in a conversation about the Christian faith. Because they ask the questions, they are more disposed to listen to the answers. And behind many a question there may be the hidden yet all-important work of the Holy Spirit, prompting that individual to seek after God.

Sometimes we may be asked a question we can't answer. It's important to be honest – and say we can't – rather than to pretend we know or to give an inadequate answer. If we can't answer, it's best to ask for time either to think it through or to ask for help. But if we've done our homework – as we've suggested earlier – more often than not we'll know how to reply to the most difficult questions because of the answers we've found God gives in the Bible. Try to use the Bible as often as you can in answering questions. What people need to receive is not our thoughts but God's Word – and it's His Word which is the living seed which produces faith in Jesus Christ leading to spiritual life.

How to be active in sharing what you believe

I hope we'll be asking at this point, 'What about other practical steps to share my faith?' Healthy Christians want to be successful in the Christian life, and that must include success in sharing their faith. Some Christians have a particular gift for evangelism, and others find it more difficult – I'm certainly one of the latter. But we're all called upon to play our part, and the more difficult we may find it the more we're cast upon God for His help – and that, paradoxically, is the secret of success.

I must begin with the obvious: *maintain close fellowship with God*. If I'm not living my life in intimate fellowship with God, I'll lose both the desire to share my faith and the ability to do so. On the other hand, when the Lord is real to me, and I'm rejoicing in all that He is to me, then there's nothing I enjoy more than talking about Him to someone else. The Book of Genesis contains a lovely description of Joseph by his father Jacob: 'Joseph is a fruitful vine, a fruitful vine near a spring, whose branches climb over a wall' (Gen. 49:22). Joseph's roots were in God. The rich resources of his life sprang from his fellowship with God. Like a tree extending its fruit-laden branches over a garden wall so that passers-by could reach its fruit and be refreshed, Joseph benefited the lives of others. So too as our roots are in the Lord Jesus, and we live close to Him, our 'branches' and 'fruit' will climb over barriers to the lives of others, and we'll benefit them. But we have to take care of our roots.

PRAY FOR OPPORTUNITIES

It's a basic principle of the Christian life, that God chooses to work for us according to our expectation. Even as I write about this I have to rebuke myself. I find that if I begin a day by asking God to help me see opportunities and to seize them, that the opportunities *do* frequently occur. If I fail to do this, however, opportunities arise often without my seeing them, or without my being prepared to seize them.

PRAY FOR INDIVIDUALS ON A REGULAR BASIS

As we live in fellowship with God, we'll find His Spirit making us concerned for particular individuals who are not yet Christians. He'll certainly do that with regard to members of our family, our colleagues at work and others. Write their names down with a view to praying for them regularly – perhaps on a daily or weekly basis. You'll be surprised at how prayer for them will make you sensitive to their needs and how opportunities will arise for you to speak to them about the Lord Jesus.

BEFRIEND PEOPLE BECAUSE OF THE LORD JESUS' LOVE FOR THEM

The Lord Jesus showed remarkable friendship to all sorts of people, and not least to the friendless. He won them by His love and concern. God will send across our path people who need our friendship; and through that friendship He may draw them to faith in His Son. I'm not suggesting that we befriend people simply with the purpose of witnessing to them. All Christians should be marked by friendliness as a spontaneous expression of Christ's love – irrespective of whether or not it leads to occasions for witness. That kind of behaviour is in itself a witness – and it pleases and honours our Lord Jesus Christ.

NEVER BE WITHOUT YOUR BIBLE

If an important part of sharing our faith is showing people from the Bible what God says and what He calls upon them to do, we should never be without the Bible if we're honestly expecting God to provide frequent possibilities for witness. We can't easily carry a whole Bible around with us, but we can have a New Testament in our jacket pocket or our handbag. I wouldn't think of going out without my wallet; I hope that I wouldn't think of going out without my New Testament. Would we believe a man was going fishing if he didn't think of taking a fishing rod?

TALK NATURALLY ABOUT YOUR INTERESTS, INCLUDING YOUR CHRISTIAN ACTIVITIES AND FAITH

Going back to work on a Monday morning after the weekend, it's usual for people to talk about what they've done. We should show an honest attentiveness to other people's interests and enjoyments. They will often ask us, 'Well, what did you do over the weekend?' Now it's easy to reply only in terms of some of the same activities they will have named, and to say, 'Oh, I took the family out on Saturday and did some gardening', and then fail to add, 'I went to church on Sunday, and we had a super After-Church Fellowship in the evening!' Now the latter half of the answer could well prompt questions that the first half wouldn't, such as, 'Do you often go to church?' Or, 'What's an After-Church Fellowship? And what happens at it?' Answers to questions such as these provide scope for witness. We shouldn't be afraid of showing that our enthusiasm for going to church at least equals that which colleagues at work show about going to watch football or rugby on a Saturday! We've even more to shout about!

INVITE PEOPLE TO CHURCH

'Faith comes from hearing the message, and the message is heard through the word of Christ' (Rom. 10:17). People are often much more ready to come to church than we give them credit for. If someone asks me why I want them to come to church with me, I answer quite honestly, 'I've put my faith in Jesus Christ, and it happened as I found Him real through listening to the teaching and preaching of God's Word, and I would like you to have that experience too.' That's God's usual way of working! Rather than invite people to your home before church for tea, it's perhaps better to invite them home afterwards for coffee or supper. If they are invited to come to your home first, it may appear as if that's a ploy to get them to church – and we should never be, or appear to be, artful or devious. If they choose to come back to your home afterwards, that may provide a key moment to talk about what they've heard – which may be exactly what they want.

READ CHRISTIAN BOOKS WHICH PRESENT THE CHRISTIAN FAITH, AND THEN GIVE THEM OR LEND THEM TO OTHERS TO READ

Not everyone enjoys reading, but some people for whom we have a spiritual responsibility will. One of the most helpful things we can do is to recommend a book, or ask them if they might like to read a book we've just been reading. If, for example, we're seen reading a book during our lunch-break, someone may well ask, 'What's that you're reading?' In telling them, we can then ask, 'Would you like to read it when I've finished?' Make a point of reading books which can be helpful to others. When you find a really good book worth passing on, it's worthwhile buying a couple so that you're always ready to pass a copy on.

NEVER WRITE ANYONE OFF AS UNLIKELY TO BE CONVERTED

A human failing is to judge too quickly by appearances. We can sympathise with Ananias who was totally surprised at the news of Saul's conversion and that the Lord wanted Ananias to be the first Christian to befriend him (Acts 9:10-16). But Saul was converted, and no doubt many Christians had been praying for God to intervene in his life. One thing we can't do is to read what's going on in people's hearts, and behind many an apparently disinterested impression that's given there's a heart that's seeking after God. What's impossible to us, certainly isn't impossible to God. Our task – to use the language of Jesus' parable of the sower – is to sow the seed wherever we can, leaving the outcome to God – and He'll give us plenty of surprises!

COMMIT EVERY DAY TO GOD AND DON'T BE ANXIOUS

The principle of Proverbs 3:6 has the widest application: 'In all your ways acknowledge him, and he will direct your paths.' Sharing our faith with others is best done spontaneously and naturally, rather than in a planned or deliberate manner. If we aim to commit ourselves to the Lord each day, and also all the people we're likely to meet – plus those whom we don't anticipate meeting – He'll make us sensitive to the opportunities and what we should say.

A PRAYER

Thank You, Father, for the people you sent across my path who spoke to me about the gospel both by their lips and by their lives. Thank You for opening my heart so that I listened to Your voice through Your Word and put my faith in Your Son as my Saviour and Lord.

I accept His commission to proclaim the good news about Him, and I want to do so with joy and enthusiasm. Please make me sensitive to the needs of others and to Your Spirit's promptings so that I may not miss the opportunities You provide. Help me to live as I should so that my conduct prompts questions about the living hope You've given me in the Lord Jesus. May I work with You to bring others to Your Son, and please give me the privilege of encouraging new Christians. For His Name's sake. Amen.

QUESTIONS

1. How would you answer the person who asks, 'Why do you feel you must share your faith with others?'
2. How have the best opportunities to share your faith come about?

BIBLE REFERENCES FOR FURTHER STUDY

THE COMMANDS GIVEN TO US TO WITNESS:
Isaiah 43:10, 11; Matthew 5:14-16; 28:19, 20; Mark 16:15; Luke 12:8, 9; Acts 1:8; 2 Corinthians 5:18-20; 2 Timothy 1:8; 1 Peter 3:15.

WHAT WE BELIEVE ABOUT
• *Faith*
John 20:29, 31; Romans 10:6-17; 1 Corinthians 2:4, 5; 2 Corinthians 5:7; Ephesians 2:8; 6:16; 1 Timothy 6:12; Hebrews 11:1,6.

• *God's existence*
Psalm 8:1, 3; 19:1-11; 139:14; John 1:1, 14, 18; 14:6-9; Acts 14:15-17; Romans 1:18-20; Hebrews 1:1-3; James 1:17.

• *God's character*
Genesis 18:25; Exodus 3:14; 34:6, 7; Psalm 86:5; 90:2; 139:3; 147:5; Isaiah 6:3; 40:18-23; Habakkuk 1:13; Malachi 3:6; John 4:24; Romans 11:33; 1 Timothy 6:15, 16; 1 John 4:8-10.

• *God's Fatherhood*
John 8:44; 14:6; 20:17; Romans 1:7; 8:15; 15:6; 2 Corinthians 1:3; 2 Thessalonians 2:16; 1 John 3:1.

• *Jesus' name*
Matthew 1:21; Luke 1:31; 2:21; Acts 4:12; Philippians 2:9-11.

• *Jesus' deity*
Isaiah 9:6; Matthew 16:16; John 1:1-4, 14, 23, 34; 5:18; 8:46;
10:30; 12:41; 20:28, 29, 31; Acts 20:28; Romans 1:4;
Colossians 2:9; 1 Peter 2:22; 2 Peter 1:16-18; 1 John 5:20.

• *Jesus' virgin conception and perfect life*
Isaiah 7:14; Matthew 1:18-24; Luke 1:26-56; 2:1-51;
2 Corinthians 5:21; Galatians 4:4, 5;
Hebrews 4:15; 1 Peter 1:19; 2:22.

• *Jesus' death*
Isaiah 53:4-6; Matthew 16:21; 20:28; 27:45-56; Mark 15:33-41;
Luke 23:44-49; John 10:11, 18; 19:28-37; Romans 3:25;
1 Corinthians 11:23-26; 2 Corinthians 5:21; Hebrews 9:26;
10:12; 1 Peter 1:18-20; 2:24; 3:18; 1 John 2:2; 4:10.

• *Jesus' descent into Hades*
1 Peter 3:19, 20.

• *Jesus' resurrection*
Matthew 16:21; 20:19; 28:1-10; Mark 16:1-8; Luke 24:1-53;
John 20:1-3; 21:1-14; Acts 1:3; 2:24; 3:15; 10:40; Romans 1:4;
1 Corinthians 15:3-8; 2 Timothy 2:8; 1 Peter 1:3, 21;
Revelation 1:18.

• *Jesus' ascension*
Psalm 110:1; Mark 16:19; Luke 24:50, 51; John 14:2;
Acts 1:1-11; Ephesians 1:19-22; 4:9, 10; 1 Timothy 3:16;
Hebrews 1:3; 10:12, 13; 1 Peter 3:22.

• *Jesus' coming again*
Daniel 7:13; Matthew 24:27, 36, 37, 44; 25:31; Luke 21:25-27;
John 14:3; Acts 3:20; 1 Corinthians 11:26; 1 Thessalonians

5:2; 2 Thessalonians 1:7-10; 1 Timothy 6:14; 1 Peter 1:13; 2 Peter 3:10; 1 John 3:2; Revelation 22:7, 12, 20.

• *Jesus' position as Judge*
Matthew 3:12; 25:31-46; Luke 3:17; 12:40-48; John 5:22, 27; Acts 10:42; 17:31; Romans 2:16; 2 Thessalonians 1:8, 9, 10; 2 Timothy 4:1; Revelation 1:7.

• *The Holy Spirit and His work*
Genesis 1:2; Psalm 139:7-13; Matthew 28:19; Luke 1:35; John 3:5, 6; John 14:16, 26; 15:26; 16:7; Acts 1:8; Romans 1:4; 8:9; 1 Corinthians 2:10; 3:16; 6:19; 12:4-11, 13; Galatians 4:6; 5:22-25; Ephesians 1:13, 14; 4:4; 6:18; 2 Thessalonians 2:13; 1 Peter 1:11, 12; 4:14; 2 Peter 1:21.

• *The Church*
Matthew 16:17, 18; Acts 20:28; 1 Corinthians 1:2; 12:14-28; 2 Corinthians 6:14-18; Galatians 6:10; Ephesians 1:22; 4:14-16; 5:21-33; 1 Timothy 3:15; Hebrews 10:21; 1 Peter 2:4, 5, 9, 10; 5:2.

• *The communion of saints*
Psalm 16:3; Malachi 3:16; Matthew 18:20; John 17:20, 21; Acts 2:42; Ephesians 4:1-6; 6:18; Colossians 3:16; 1 Thessalonians 5:11; Hebrews 10:24, 25; 12:1, 22-24; 1 John 1:3, 7.

• *The forgiveness of sins*
Psalm 32:1, 2, 5; Isaiah 44:22; Matthew 6:12; 26:28; Mark 2:5, 7; Luke 7:48, 50; Acts 2:38; 3:19; 5:31; 10:43; Ephesians 1:7; 4:32; Colossians 1:13, 14; Hebrews 9:22; 1 John 1:8, 9; 2:2, 12.

• *The resurrection of the body:*
Isaiah 26:19; Daniel 12:2; Matthew 22:29-32; John 5:28, 29; 6:39, 40, 44; Acts 4:2; 24:15; 1 Corinthians 15:12-58; 2 Corinthians 4:14; 1 Thessalonians 4:14, 16, 17; Philippians 3:20, 21; 1 Peter 1:3; 1 John 3:2; Revelation 20:11-15.

- *Everlasting life:*

John 3:16, 36; 4:14; 6:27, 40, 47, 54, 68; 10:28; 11:26;
Romans 6:22, 23; Galatians 6:8; Philippians 1:21, 23;
1 Timothy 1:16; 6:12; 2 Timothy 1:10; Titus 1:2;
Hebrews 5:9; 1 Peter 5:10; 2 Peter 1:11; 1 John 5:11-13.

7

Aim at proper goals!

If we aim at nothing, we're fairly certain to achieve it! Although so obvious it's nevertheless true that the neglect of specific goals explains many a failure in the Christian life and lack of spiritual achievement.

Without goals we tend to be aimless, and without a yardstick we fail to determine whether we're making spiritual headway. David in the Old Testament and Paul in the New stand out as men of solid spiritual achievement. Significantly, they both knew what they wanted when it came to their relationship with God. David declared, 'One thing I ask of the Lord, this is what I seek: that I may dwell in the house of the Lord all the days of my life, to gaze upon the beauty of the Lord and to seek him in his temple' (Ps. 27:4). David wanted more of God Himself. He reckoned knowing God to be his most prized possession.

Paul expressed himself similarly, 'But one thing I do: forgetting what is behind and straining towards what is ahead, I press on toward the goal to win the prize for which God has called me heavenwards in Christ Jesus' (Phil. 3:13, 14); and that goal – as the preceding verses show – was knowing Jesus Christ. Only as we establish proper goals do we point our life and energies in the right direction.

Numerous legitimate objectives might be suggested for the Christian, but we'll aim to cover the principal ones. And there's no doubt where we should start and to which we should give most attention, since at the top of the list there's the goal at which David and Paul aimed.

KNOWING GOD

The essence – the most important part – of the eternal life God gives us through His Son Jesus Christ is knowing Him. Praying to His Father prior to His crucifixion, the Lord Jesus said, 'Now this is eternal life: that they may know you, the only true God, and Jesus Christ, whom you have sent' (John 17:3). Eternal life brings many wonderful benefits, but knowing God is the greatest. To know our Creator is our highest end as creatures made originally in the image of God our Creator.

The first chapters of the Bible describe man living in the closest possible fellowship with his Maker. God brought the beasts of the field and the birds of the air to man to name (Gen. 2:19). God walked in the Garden of Eden in the cool of the day (Gen. 3:8), and man enjoyed God's fellowship without fear. But tragically sin spoiled all this, and man had to be shut out of the Garden of Eden (Gen. 3:24). The good news of the gospel is that God's wonderful plan of salvation completely reverses this sad and tragic situation, and the Book of Revelation describes how everything is going to end up for God's people. John heard a voice saying, 'Now the dwelling of God is with men, and he will live with them. They will be his people, and God himself will be with them and be their God' (Rev. 21:3). God wants us to know Him better here and now, and eternal life will be the glorious completion of what has begun for us in this life since we put our faith in Jesus Christ.

How then are we to get to know God? The question has a three-fold answer. First and foremost, we get to know God through our Lord Jesus Christ. He alone is the Son of God, the Word who became flesh and lived for a while among us (John 1:14). It's in Him that we see God's glory, for He is the visible image of the invisible God. God the Father has determined that His Son shall be the sole means of His final self-revelation to the world. If we would know God, it must be through His Son. There is no other way (John 14:6). While the Father and the Son – together with the Holy Spirit – are distinct Persons, we should not draw a dis-tinction between knowing the Father and knowing the Son. As we know the Son, we also know the Father since the Son is the Father's perfect image. This explains why Paul could write, 'What is more, I consider everything a loss compared to the surpassing greatness of knowing Christ Jesus my Lord' (Phil. 3:8).

We come then, secondly, to the important place of the Scriptures, the Bible, in our knowing God. It is through the Scriptures that we get to know Jesus Christ. It is in the Scriptures that we have the four gospels, four different yet complementary accounts of the life and ministry of our Lord Jesus. They also provide us with His words and teaching. The Acts of the Apostles goes on to describe what the Lord Jesus continued to do through His body, the church, after His ascension, and the letters – which make up the rest of the New Testament – all focus in different ways upon what it means to be united to Jesus Christ. The Old Testament similarly focuses upon our Lord Jesus: the Spirit of the Lord Jesus in the prophets 'predicted the sufferings of Christ and the glories that would follow' (1 Pet. 1:11).

The Lord Jesus is the centre of God's revelation in both testaments of the Bible (cf. Luke 24:27), and He's the key to our understanding of them (John 5:39). They are, therefore, the principal means God uses to help us to know Him. If we neglect the Scriptures, we immediately hinder our growth in our knowledge of God. Whether it's our private reading of the Bible or our listening to the preaching of God's Word, God's purpose is that through these means we should know Him better. To realise this whets our appetite for both.

But there's a third factor in our knowing God which is all-important: the ministry of the Third Person of the Trinity, God the Holy Spirit. He lives within every Christian – in fact, it's impossible to be a Christian and not to have received the gift of the Holy Spirit (Rom. 8:9). His special ministry, of which He never tires, is to take from what belongs to the Lord Jesus and make it known to us (John 16:15). His ability to do this is absolutely unique since He is God, and as the Spirit of God He alone searches the deep things of God (1 Cor. 2:10). He always has fresh light to throw upon the Scriptures to increase our understanding and to deepen our knowledge of God.

We've considered then three essential principles for growing in our knowledge of our Saviour: first, concentrate upon the Person and Work of Jesus Christ; second, give careful attention to the whole of God's Word; and, third, always depend upon the Holy Spirit for understanding and illumination.

There's a world of difference between knowing *about* someone and actually knowing them; and the same is true of our knowledge of God and of His Son Jesus Christ. The way in which we grow in our personal knowledge of God as Christians isn't complicated. First, we learn a truth about Him, and then – by an exercise of faith – we respond to that truth and discover its reality experimentally. Let me give an example. There are often times when I feel weak and inadequate, perhaps because some task appears too big for me. But early on in my Christian life

I learned that the Lord Jesus wants to be the secret strength of those who trust in Him, and so more times than I can count I've responded to that fact, and I've said to myself, in the face of difficulties, 'I can do everything through him who gives me strength' (Phil. 4:13). And it works! The Lord Jesus always keeps His promise, and I prove and *know* Him to be my strength.

Secondly, we know God by enjoying fellowship with Him. Fellowship with God isn't only praying to Him and asking Him for things. It's also sharing our lives with Him and sometimes just pouring out our hearts to Him, telling Him how we see things, with the desire to gain His perspective upon our life.

An important principle taught in the Bible applies here to our knowing God: 'Whoever has will be given more; whoever does not have, even what he has will be taken from him' (Mark 4:25). We can't stand still in our knowing God: we either go forwards or backwards. The key to progress is obedience – something we'll look at in greater detail later. Each time God graciously makes Himself known to us and speaks to us through His Word, it's vital that we respond positively. As we respond, we increase our capacity for knowing Him; if we resist, then we decrease our capacity and become impoverished Christians.

It's not difficult to judge whether or not we are growing in our knowledge of God. If we are, we'll be delighting in His Word and in His Son, aware of the Holy Spirit applying the Scriptures to our lives, and we'll be loving God more and more for Himself rather than simply for His many gifts.

As the most important goal – which is why we're giving most attention to it – it's the goal which will be under greatest attack by our enemy, Satan. Watch out for those things – and perhaps friendships – that spoil your fellowship with God, and be honest enough to deal with them ruthlessly. At the same time actively pursue activities and friendships which foster your fellowship with God and your knowledge of Him, such as regular prayer and Bible reading, meeting with other Christians, corporate prayer and the reading of Christian books. Be determined to follow on to know the Lord – it's the goal above all goals for the Christian.

MATURITY OF FAITH

Spiritual maturity is closely related to our primary goal – knowing God. Knowing Him transforms our way of thinking and, as a result, the way we live. One of the foremost marks of Christian maturity is the achievement of balance, whether in a balanced view of Christian doctrines, or in a balanced life which avoids unhelpful extremes.

But, in particular, spiritual maturity is maturity of faith. It may be equated with being strong, firm and steadfast in the faith (1 Pet. 5:10). From beginning to end the Christian life is one of faith, a fact of which it's important not to lose sight. Think of how your faith came to birth. Probably in a variety of ways God brought before you the Person of His Son, Jesus Christ, and there came a moment when you realised how trustworthy He is and that God was calling you to put your confidence in Jesus as your Saviour. That was but the *beginning* of faith.

When faith begins, it's small. Its strength is not in its size but in the One upon whom it rests. It grows, first, through knowing more of the One in whom it trusts – and we've rightly put knowing God as our primary goal.

Faith also grows through exercise. It's rather like a muscle – the more you use it properly the stronger it becomes. This provides part of the explanation for the trials and difficulties God permits. It's not the explanation of all our testings but it's certainly the use to which God turns them if we'll co-operate with Him. (Heb. 11 records the many testings that came to Old Testament believers, and, significantly, they all profited from them as they responded with faith.) If we're wise, therefore, we won't resent testings and difficulties, but we'll aim to respond with faith. False faith collapses when the going's tough, but genuine faith stands.

Faith needs to be put to work. Like a lively and active child, it has to be doing things. Knowing what it's right to expect God to do for us, faith trusts Him for those things and asks Him specifically for them. This isn't something airy-fairy, but it's down to earth and practical. For example, it's easy to spend our lives worrying about a roof over our heads, what we're going to eat and wear and how long we're likely to live. But faith takes God at His Word (Matt. 6:25-34), and puts God's kingdom and His righteousness first and leaves it to God to take care of these practical issues – and He does! Faith at work means we seek God's kingdom and righteousness first in our career. If we're to get promotion, it won't be because we manipulate people or cultivate special relationships in order to bring us favour but because we honour God and do our work for Him. Putting faith to work means trusting God to bring us the right marriage partner if marriage is His will for us.

The enemy of our souls hates to see us trusting God, and his unceasing aim is to get us to take our eyes off God, so that we live by what our eyes see rather than by the unseen realities. But the virtue he attacks is the virtue to use against him! 'Take up the shield of faith,' Paul urges, 'with which you can extinguish all the flaming arrows of the evil one' (Eph. 6:16). Faith represents our invincible shield against Satan and all his weaponry. When faith is under attack, I find great encouragement in remembering that my faith is precious to God, and that His final purpose is that my faith should be proved genuine through difficulties so that in the end it may result in praise, glory and honour when the Lord Jesus returns (1 Pet. 1:7).

THE FULL EXPERIENCE OF SALVATION

Salvation is a Bible word for which there's no satisfactory substitute. When God first helps us to understand our peril because of sin, salvation becomes a meaningful word. Convicted of his sin, the Philippian jailer called out, 'What must I do to be saved?' Only the Holy Spirit could have given him such discernment of his need, and the Christian missionaries knew there was but one answer, 'Believe in the Lord Jesus, and you will be saved – you and your household' (Acts 16:30, 31).

Salvation has three tenses: *I have been saved* from the guilt and penalty of sin because I've repented and put my faith in the Lord Jesus Christ; *I am being saved* here and now from the power of sin by the help of the Holy Spirit, God's gift to me in the Lord Jesus; and *I shall be saved* from the actual presence of sin as I enter ultimately into the full enjoyment of eternal life and all its benefits. These three tenses impress upon me that conversion is but the beginning of my experience of salvation. They also remind me that salvation should be a present experience: moment by moment God wants me to know His deliverance from the power of sin.

When we first become Christians, it's wonderful to know the great sense of release that our sins have been completely forgiven – and forgotten – by God. But a feeling of horror may soon follow as we realise that we still sin. We don't sin as once we did – carelessly and for the most part unconsciously. Now when we sin we are usually immediately aware of it and very unhappy about it. Overwhelmed by our feelings of sinfulness, we may ask ourselves, 'Can I really be a Christian if I sin like this?' I can recall months of torment, soon after I became a Christian, which I didn't share with anyone, because of the acute battle I found myself fighting with sin and temptation.

But we shouldn't be surprised at this growing awareness of sin. The explanation is quite simple: God's light has come into our lives, and His light shows up our darkness and wrongs and evils which previously we wouldn't have noticed. In fact, the closer we live to God, the more aware we'll be of everything that's incompatible with His light or holiness. We find a helpful illustration of this experience in three of Paul's letters. 1 Corinthians was one of his early letters, and in it he describes himself as 'the least of the apostles' (1 Cor. 15:9). Ephesians was written later, in the middle of his ministry, and in it he describes himself as 'the least of all God's people' (Eph. 3:8). But writing to Timothy, towards the end of his life, he wrote of himself as 'the worst' of sinners (1 Tim. 1:15). Now that wasn't going backwards in Christian experience, but forwards!

Two practices are important if our experience of salvation is to be daily. First, we must act upon God's promise of forgiveness, a promise summed up in 1 John 1:9: 'If we confess our sins, he is faithful and just and will forgive us our sins and purify us from all unrighteousness.' As soon as we become aware that we may have grieved God, we should confess it to Him and be specific, where possible, in acknowledging where and how we have sinned. God's promise of forgiveness demands that we confess not simply our sin but our *sins*. As I honestly tell God what I know my sin to be, I grow to hate it more and to turn from it more resolutely.

Second, we must ask God for the help of the Holy Spirit and be obedient to Him as we discover what God wants for our life. Romans 8, verses 1 and 2, provide wonderful assurance and an important principle: 'Therefore, there is now no condemnation for those who are in Christ Jesus, because through Christ Jesus the law of the Spirit of life set me free from the law of sin and death'. Our grasp of the meaning of the second verse is probably helped if we substitute the word 'principle' for 'law'. Before my conversion I knew the downward pull of the principle of sin which lives within me, and I had no power to overcome it. But on my conversion I received the Holy Spirit – the Spirit of life – and He introduced a new principle into my life – a principle of power setting me free from the old principle of sin leading to death. Think of a car going up a hill. All the time it goes up there's the downward pull of gravity which would make you argue that the car ought to go down. But, in fact, the car goes up the hill because another, and greater principle, is at work at the same time – the principle of power through an internal combustion engine under the car's bonnet. So it is in the Christian life.

I sometimes become weary of my battle against sin and despair at my slowness to learn lessons of victory as quickly as I ought. But I constantly remind myself that it's a *good* fight, and I think of the future aspect of salvation when I'll be freed from the actual presence of sin altogether. Like a runner finding fresh wind as he sees the finishing line in sight, so I find strength for my present battle against sin as I realise that the end is in sight.

THE FULLNESS OF THE HOLY SPIRIT

Throughout this book we've made constant reference to the work and ministry of God the Holy Spirit. He is that other 'Counsellor' (John 14:16) whose task it is to be to us all that the Lord Jesus was to His disciples when He was physically present with them. The Holy Spirit would never have us focus our attention upon Him but rather upon the Lord Jesus Christ. But that clear fact must not mean that we neglect an important goal which the New Testament sets before us and which is essential for the achievement of all the other goals we are considering. That goal is summed up in Ephesians 5:18: 'Be filled with the Spirit.' The tense implies not a once-for-all happening but a constantly renewed experience.

To be filled with the Spirit is to be aware of God's presence and involvement in our life. To be filled with the Spirit is to enjoy the Spirit's full assistance – the full benefit of His counsel, His intercession and the fellowship into which He would bring us with God and other Christians. To be filled with the Spirit is to be controlled by Him – for all our faculties and powers to be subject to His influence. It's equal to letting Him have full possession of us. To be filled with the Spirit is to be a reflection of the Lord Jesus Christ. The world desperately needs to see the Lord Jesus and to understand who He is and what He does in people's lives. When the Holy Spirit, who is the Spirit of Jesus Christ, fills us, then Jesus fills our lives. A Spirit-filled life has the capacity to make others thirsty for the Lord Jesus and to bring them to Him to drink for themselves (John 7:37-39).

The experience of the early Christians, described in the Acts of the Apostles, best illustrates what it means to be filled with the Spirit. Filled with the Spirit, they exercised their God-given gifts (2:4), answered effectively the questions put to them (4:8) and were bold in their witness (4:31). Filled with the Spirit, they were endued with wisdom (6:3), spiritual vision (7:55), faith (11:24) and remarkable discernment (13:9, 10). The sad thing is that we may not be enjoying these benefits ourselves. The Holy Spirit is a Person, not a thing, and He may be grieved. When we grieve the Holy Spirit, we forfeit our experience of His fellowship and power. Two people can live together in the same house, but fail to know the benefits of living together because they aren't in harmony. If we're out of harmony with the Holy Spirit, although He lives within us, He won't be filling our lives. He will permit no tolerance of evil and no indifference to the things God hates.

I've come to appreciate that God intends us to come to Him for the infilling of His Spirit whenever we're aware of our need of His help – as often as we feel empty of boldness, wisdom, spiritual vision, faith or discernment or whatever else it may be.

The Lord Jesus put it so simply and clearly, 'Which of you fathers, if your son asks for a fish, will give him a snake instead? Or if he asks for an egg, will give him a scorpion? If you then, though you are evil, know how to give good gifts to your children, how much more will your Father in heaven give the Holy Spirit to those who ask him!' (Luke 11:11-13). The Lord Jesus also used the picture of thirst (John 7:37-39) as we've seen. As often as I feel the need of the Spirit's infilling I should confidently ask God for what He commands.

LIKENESS TO JESUS CHRIST

It's helpful to have a picture in our mind of God's purpose for our life, so that we may make it a clear goal. Picture a sculptor. He has his subject before him, and he also has a lump of stone and his chisel. The subject, in our case, is the Lord Jesus. We are the lump of stone and the Holy Spirit is the sculptor with His chisel. His objective is to make us in character like the Lord Jesus.

By new birth we've become God's sons and daughters. Having adopted us into His family, God's declared purpose is that we should 'be conformed to the likeness of his Son' (Rom. 8:29), who 'is the radiance of God's glory and the exact representation of his being' (Heb. 1:3). It all makes such good sense: in the beginning man bore the perfect image of God his Creator, but that image was marred by man's rebellion; through our union with Jesus Christ that image is renewed and restored.

God wants us to be like His Son in character, attitudes and actions. It's a goal to set before us every day, without exception. The New Testament constantly says to us things such as, 'Your attitude should be the same as that of Christ Jesus ...' (Phil. 2:5), 'Live a life of love, just as Christ loved us ...' (Eph. 5:2), and 'Christ suffered for you, leaving you an example, that you should follow in his steps' (1 Pet. 2:21).

God the Holy Spirit supervises this change and accomplishes it. Changing the picture from the sculptor with his chisel, He's the divine Gardener who is concerned for the growth of specific fruit in us: 'The fruit of the Spirit is love, joy, peace, patience, kindness, goodness, faithfulness, gentleness and self-control' (Gal. 5:22). If we add up the Spirit's fruit, like an arithmetic sum, the answer is plain: it's the character of Jesus Christ. Notice it's not the *fruits* of the Spirit that we've read about but the *fruit*. There is a distinction: when the Holy Spirit works in us He intends to produce the whole fruit, not just parts of it. He aims at our total likeness to Jesus Christ.

Fruit grows only as a tree receives proper nourishment and appropriate pruning. God the Holy Spirit is most concerned about our spiritual feeding upon God's Word and our growing fellowship first with God and then with other Christians – these privileges are indispensable for fruitfulness. As the divine Gardener He also prunes our lives by means of difficulties and hardships in order to produce a better harvest. Fruit always has its own delightful fragrance and attractiveness. As we become more like the Lord Jesus, we become a fragrance of Him in the world (2 Cor. 2:14), and we draw attention not to ourselves but to His power to transform lives.

We may often pray, 'Lord, make me like Your Son', and it's right that we should. But we may be in for surprises as God takes us at our word and accomplishes this purpose in ways we wouldn't expect, and not least by 'pruning' experiences.

THE PRACTICE OF OBEDIENCE

I want to stress the word 'practice' because obedience is an activity of our will which must be constantly maintained. Our experience of salvation began when we first responded to God's call to repent and believe on His Son: we obeyed – and everything happened as God promised. Wherever we turn in the Bible we find it stated that obedience is the secret of success if we want to please God. Psalm 1, for example, sets the stage for the whole book of Psalms and describes the happiness of the man who genuinely pleases God and whose life is fruitful. His secret is simple: 'His delight is in the law of the Lord, and on his law he meditates day and night' (v. 2). The longest psalm – Psalm 119 – also majors on obedience, almost in every verse, and in it David asks a crucial question and then gives the answer, 'How can a young man keep his way pure? By living according to your word' (v. 9).

Faced with the awesome task of taking over from Moses, Joshua was naturally anxious about his ability to be successful, and God reassured him in these words: 'Be careful to obey all the law my servant Moses gave you; do not turn from it to the right or to the left, that you may be successful wherever you go. Do not let this Book of the Law depart from your mouth; meditate on it day and night, so that you may be careful to do everything written in it. Then you will be prosperous and successful' (Josh. 1:7, 8). The Lord Jesus placed exactly the same emphasis on obedience: 'You are my friends if you do what I command' (John 15:14).

We are unlikely to live a single day without the Holy Spirit somehow or other prompting our conscience to action. When we read God's Word or hear it taught, He'll urge us to obey it. Our obedience should be thoughtful and precise. Partial obedience is not really obedience at all. We practise obedience as we live in the light of truth we already know and as we respond to new truth that's brought before us. Obedience to old and familiar truth is as important as obedience to new truth. What a difference there would be in our lives if we were obedient to what we *already* know of God's will, quite apart from what we still need to discover.

God delights in our joyful obedience. He's not grudging in His love towards us, and we shouldn't be grudging in our obedience to Him because 'His commands are not burdensome' (1 John 5:3). The key to joyful obedience is loving our Lord Jesus Christ. When our love for Him grows as it ought, obedience becomes our delight and joy. Whenever I find obedience at all difficult I should check my fellowship with the Lord Jesus Christ and the love I feel for Him. Again we see how much our goals are related: the more I know the Lord Jesus Christ, the more I'll love Him; and the more I love Him, the more I'll trust Him and obey Him.

We need to be practical and down to earth in our approach to obedience. When we read the Scriptures in private or when we are about to listen to preaching, it's helpful to pray, 'Lord, what do you want me to do?' The Lord won't allow that question to go unanswered. It's an asset to write down in a notebook the truths we feel we're learning and calls to obedience that God gives us. Writing them down serves to fix them in our memory, and it makes it easy to review our progress. Review is important because the natural perversity of our hearts means that we may shirk the full implications of obedience in some sensitive issue.

The exciting benefit of obedience is that it's the open sesame to knowing our Lord Jesus Christ better, and thus of a growing faith in Him which, in turn, leads to increased obedience – and that's how we grow as Christians. The Lord Jesus promises that as we obey Him, He will show Himself to us and that both the Father and He will make their home with us (John 14:21, 23): such promises are the best incentives to obedience that I know!

THE USE OF OUR GIFTS IN GOD'S SERVICE

We all possess both natural gifts and spiritual gifts. That doesn't mean that we are aware of them all as yet. For some of us the future is going to be a time of great discovery. Natural gifts – whether of public speaking, music, art, aptitude with our hands and so on – are not to be despised, and they may well have a spiritual usefulness. In addition we'll all have a spiritual gift or gifts. Spiritual gifts are the gift of the Spirit, given 'just as He determines' (1 Cor. 12:11), for 'the common good' (1 Cor. 12:7). It's not wrong to expect to have God-given gifts that can be employed in His service. We are right to be fearful of pride and self-importance, but we mustn't go to the other extreme. The advice to follow is that given in Romans 12:3: 'Do not think of yourself more highly than you ought, but rather think of yourself with sober judgment, in accordance with the measure of faith God has given you'.

Three passages in the New Testament describe spiritual gifts – Romans 12, 1 Corinthians 12 and 1 Peter 4:8-11. The tremendous variety ranges from the ability to proclaim God's Word to the practical gift of hospitality. All gifts develop by use, and if we don't exercise a God-given gift we'll find our ability to use it decreases.

The discovery of our gifts requires the use of our common sense. First, we should pray that God will show us our gifts by causing them to become obvious as we seek to obey Him. Second, we should look honestly at ourselves and decide what we enjoy doing most and what we're obviously better at than at other things. We should also be guided by circumstances because God orders them as we're obedient to Him. It's appropriate that we should ask our spiritual leaders if they have any convictions about our best contribution for the common good of the body of Christ.

Using our gifts as the Bible counsels, we will place the emphasis upon serving others in the ways they need rather than simply doing what we enjoy. We will use our gifts in dependence upon God's ability rather than upon our own, and, remembering that it's through His grace that we have any gifts at all, we will honestly seek that God will be praised and not us. Never despise any piece of service you are invited to do. Experience proves that God's pattern is invariably that one piece of service leads to another, and often a lesser opportunity to a greater.

THE ONLY PRIZE OR REWARD THAT MATTERS – JESUS CHRIST'S APPROVAL

Motivation has much to do with the successful achievement of right goals. The proper motivation behind all the goals we've mentioned is this final one – the ultimate commendation Jesus Christ will give to those who please Him.

If we think of ourselves as stewards of our Master's property – a frequent picture in the New Testament – then our Master's approval is what we should be eagerly seeking. The glorious prospect before the Christian is the hope (assurance) of our Lord Jesus Christ's return – something we'll talk about in our last chapter – and we should aim not to be a disappointment to Him when the time arrives for Him to evaluate our service.

The early Christians set this exciting goal before them. Peter urged those who had been given responsibility for others to serve the Lord with the awareness that when the Chief Shepherd appears they would 'receive the crown of glory that will never fade away' (1 Pet. 5:4). Paul referred to this motivation constantly (1 Cor. 9:24 ff; 2 Cor. 5:9; 1 Thess. 2:19): 'The time has come for my departure. I have fought the good fight, I have finished the race, I have kept the faith. Now there is in store for me the crown of righteousness, which the Lord, the righteous Judge, will award to me on that day – and not only to me, but also to all who have longed for his appearing' (2 Tim. 4:6-8).

The Lord Jesus laid stress in His parables upon the prize that really counts. To the good and faithful servant, for example, the

Master says, 'Well done, good and faithful servant! You have been faithful with a few things; I will put you in charge of many things. Come and share your master's happiness' (Matt. 25:21). Jesus Christ's approval of our lives and service is what matters. When this is our motivation, we won't live to please ourselves – our pleasure will be what gives Him pleasure. We won't live simply with an eye to the approval of others. Not that we won't want to please other people, but that won't be our prime motive. We'll avoid the peril of being men-pleasers by means of our superior aim to please Jesus Christ.

The world may regard such a goal as foolishness, but it's far from that. All other rewards that men and women may aim at will pass away with the course of time, but the reward Jesus Christ gives is eternal. 'He's no fool who loses what he cannot keep to gain what he cannot lose' (Jim Elliot).

Worthwhile goals are never achieved without discipline. If an athlete is to achieve anything noteworthy, he sets himself goals for each day which will involve strict self-discipline about hours of sleep, diet and training. When a soldier enlists, he's immediately subject to discipline – his whole training is calculated to make self-discipline second nature to him. When a farmer desires a harvest, he has to discipline himself to go out in all weathers to sow, water and feed his crops in order to have a harvest to reap. Significantly, as we've seen earlier, these three pictures – the athlete, the soldier, and the farmer – are used to describe the Christian as he ought to be (2 Tim. 2:3-6). Discipline is never easy, but to state that it's worth it all is a great understatement!

A PRAYER

Lord, I want to thank You for giving me purpose and specific goals for my life, through the faith You've given me in Your Son. Deliver me from settling for anything less than knowing You better day by day and becoming more like the Lord Jesus in my character, attitudes and behaviour. With Your help, I commit myself to obeying Your Son and to using all my gifts in the service of others as You choose. Whatever else is true of my life, may it end with my hearing the Lord Jesus say, 'Well done!' For His Name's sake. Amen.

QUESTIONS

1. In what areas of ordinary life has it been important to you to have goals? What have you found helpful in achieving them? Are the lessons you've learned as a result applicable to your Christian life?

2. Do some spiritual goals seem more difficult to achieve than others? If so, why? What should be our response with regard to the more difficult goals?

BIBLE REFERENCES FOR FURTHER STUDY

KNOWING GOD:

Psalm 25:14; Proverbs 1:7; 2:1-5; Jeremiah 31:34; Amos 3:3; John 14:7-11, 17; 17:3; 1 Corinthians 13:12; Ephesians 1:17; Colossians 1:10; 1 John 2:3; 4:7, 8; 5:20.

MATURITY OF FAITH:

Romans 4:18-21; 5:1-5; 12:3, 6; 2 Corinthians 5:7; Galatians 2:20; 5:6; Ephesians 3:12, 17; 6:16; Colossians 1:23; 2:5-7; 1 Thessalonians 1:3; 2 Thessalonians 1:3; 1 Timothy 6:12; Hebrews 10:22; 11:1-40; 12:1-11; James 1:2-4; 2:14-26; 1 Peter 1:6, 7; 5:10; 2 Peter 1:5-9.

THE FULL EXPERIENCE OF SALVATION:

John 7:37-39; 8:36; 12:24-26; 14:21, 23; Romans 5:1-5; 6:1-14; Galatians 2:20; Ephesians 4:20-24; 6:10-18; Colossians 3:5-17; 2 Thessalonians 2:13-17; 2 Timothy 4:7, 8; Revelation 3:20.

THE FULLNESS OF THE HOLY SPIRIT:

Luke 4:1; 11:11-13; John 7:37-39; Acts 2:4; 4:8, 31; 5:32; 6:3, 5, 8; 7:55; 9:17; 11:24; 13:9, 10, 52; Romans 15:13; Ephesians 4:30; 5:18-20; 1 Thessalonians 5:19.

LIKENESS TO JESUS CHRIST:

Matthew 11:28-30; 16:24; John 13:1-17; Acts 7:59, 60; Romans 8:29; 13:14; 15:1-3; 2 Corinthians 3:18; Galatians 5:22, 23; Ephesians 4:13; 5:2; Philippians 2:5-8; 3:10; 1 Peter 2:21; 1 John 2:6; 3:3.

THE PRACTICE OF OBEDIENCE:

Joshua 1:7, 8; 11:15; 22:5; Psalm 1:1-3; Matthew 7:21, 24-27; 12:50; Luke 11:28; John 14:15, 21, 23; 15:10, 14; Romans 1:5; 6:16, 17; Galatians 5:7; Philippians 2:12, 13; James 1:22-25; 1 John 2:3-6; 3:21-24; 5:2, 3.

THE USE OF OUR GIFTS IN GOD'S SERVICE:

Romans 12:1-8; 1 Corinthians 12:1-31; Ephesians 4:1-16; 1 Peter 4:8-11.

THE ONLY PRIZE OR REWARD THAT MATTERS:

Matthew 5:12; 25:14-46; Luke 19:11-27; 1 Corinthians :24-27; 2 Corinthians 4:16-18; Philippians 3:10, 11, 14; Colossians 3:1-4, 23, 24; 1 Thessalonians 2:19, 20; 2 Timothy 2:3, 4; 4:7, 8; Hebrews 6:9-12; James 1:12; 1 Peter 5:4; 2 Peter 1:10, 11; Revelation 14:13; 22:12.

8

Getting to grips
with the Bible!

Bible study isn't an end in itself. But the obedience we rightly give
to the Lord Jesus Christ – the great proof of our love for Him – can
increase only as we grow in our understanding of His will through
the Bible (often called 'the Word of God' or 'the Scriptures').

Getting to grips with the Bible requires hard work and our best
effort. 'Do your best,' Paul urged Timothy, 'to present yourself to
God as one approved, a workman who does not need to be ashamed
and who correctly handles the word of truth' (2 Tim. 2:15). The
most rewarding returns come to those who are prepared to give their
best to it. But the treasures and benefits it yields are incomparable.
Initially it seems a tremendous task, and it is, in fact, the work of
a lifetime. Don't allow yourself to be put off, however, by how vast
an assignment it seems to be. Even as a journey of a thousand miles
begins with the first step, so knowing the Bible requires a simple
beginning, followed by persistent daily effort.

THE SUPREME OBJECTIVE
The supreme objective of all Bible study must be to know God
through His Son, Jesus Christ. When we constantly remind

ourselves of this, we avoid the snare of Bible study becoming an end in itself. The Lord Jesus Christ is the Living Word, through whom God speaks to us as through no one else (John 1:1; Heb. 1:1, 2). The Lord Jesus, the Living Word, communicates to us through the written Word which His Spirit inspired (1 Pet. 1:10-12).

The Lord Jesus Himself is the key to the Bible. Knowing Him is the unique key with which to open its treasures. He is the truth and reality behind all the Old Testament types and shadows. He's the focus of God's eternal purposes. He's at the centre of God's New Covenant – in the Old Testament He is partly hidden, and in the New He is fully revealed. He's the meeting place of all God's promises, and in Him they are 'Yes' and 'Amen' (2 Cor. 1:20). Even the Scripture genealogies are important because they show the human lineage of the divine Saviour. The laws of the Bible function as a schoolmaster to bring us to Christ because they show us our need of a Saviour. The good news the Bible proclaims is His gospel, by which we're drawn into wonderful union and communion with Him.

It's no exaggeration to say that the Lord Jesus Himself is the reality, the centre of interest and the scope of the whole of the Scriptures. Loving the Lord Jesus, therefore, we soon find ourselves loving the Bible – and unashamedly so. When we stop loving the Scriptures, it almost certainly indicates that something has happened to dull our love for Him. Our subject of getting to grips with the Bible is basic to our discipleship.

UNDERSTAND WHAT THE BIBLE IS

The Bible is God's Word. 'All Scripture is God-breathed' (2 Tim. 3:16). Those who wrote the Scriptures were men who 'spoke from God as they were carried along by the Holy Spirit' (2 Pet. 1:21). The Bible yields its secrets only to those who are prepared to approach it with reverence – with their shoes off their feet – and with the desire to obey God in whatever He may say to them through its pages. If we forget that the Bible is God's Word, then we'll soon find our understanding of it limited and our appetite for it diminished. I find it helpful to remind myself that when I open the Bible and read it I'm coming into the immediate presence of the King of kings, and that I do so in order to listen to His voice so that I may then go out to do what pleases Him.

The Bible is the food our soul most requires. Born again of God's Spirit, our souls have been cleansed by the blood of our Lord Jesus, and they are alive to God. As our bodies require nourishment, so our souls require the food which the Bible provides. Our souls are especially fed by it as it provides glimpses of our Lord Jesus Christ. As we read the Bible we'll find the Holy Spirit taking the things that belong to Christ and our union with Him and making them alive and meaningful to our souls.

The Bible also brings spiritual strength by its promises. We'll be regularly lifted above difficulties as God's promises are made relevant to our immediate situation. We'll pray, 'Strengthen me according to your word' (Ps. 119:28), and it will happen (Phil. 4:13)! The Bible has a unique ability to renew our spiritual life and our general sense of well-being. David testified, 'I will never forget your precepts, for by them you have renewed my life' (Ps. 119:93). The Bible makes our conscience aware of how we may please God and avoid the things which displease Him. 'I have hidden your word in my heart,' David wrote, 'that I might not sin against you' (Ps. 119:11).

The Bible is a principal weapon in our fight against sin, temptation and Satan. The benefits reading and studying the Bible bring explain why Satan, the enemy of our souls, does his wicked best to hinder and distract us from getting to grips with the Bible. If you think of a soldier without a weapon, you have an apt picture of a Christian who neglects the Bible. 'Take ... the sword of the Spirit, which is the word of God' (Eph. 6:17), Paul urges. If the devil succeeds in making us neglect the Bible, we've allowed a vital weapon against him to slip from our grasp.

Our Lord Jesus Christ was tempted by the devil immediately after His baptism. The devil came to Him with all sorts of subtle suggestions, each calculated to turn Him away from obedience to His Father. Our Lord's answer on each occasion – like the quick thrust of a sword – was to quote appropriate Scriptures. Significantly, the devil also quoted Scriptures to our Lord, but always out of context. When Satan endeavours to sow doubts in our minds, the Scriptures provide an unfailing answer. The Bible teaches us how to recognise Satan's devices and to withstand him successfully.

The Bible is the means by which God equips us for every kind of good work. The more we know the Bible the more we discover how adequately it provides principles to guide us in all aspects of daily life. Because it is God-breathed, it 'is useful for teaching, rebuking, correcting and training in righteousness, so that the man of God may be thoroughly equipped for every good work' (2 Tim. 3:16-18). It's a lamp to our feet and a light to our path (Ps. 119:105). As we know and obey the Scriptures, our characters are daily moulded by God, and our Lord Jesus Christ's rule as King is maintained and extended in our lives.

ASK FOR THE HELP OF THE HOLY SPIRIT

Without God's help, we are as unable to read the Bible with understanding as we are unable to read a sundial if the sun isn't shining. The Holy Spirit, who caused the Scriptures to be written, is given to every Christian to teach and instruct him in the things of God. If we take His help for granted, we'll probably lose it, but if we ask for it with humility we'll receive it in plenty. Spiritual understanding isn't a question of intellectual ability but a matter of submissive wills and minds bowing before God as the Scriptures are studied, with the Holy Spirit as our Teacher. David's prayers are an example to us: 'Open my eyes that I may see wonderful things in your law ... Let me understand the teaching of your precepts' (Ps. 119:18, 27). Make it a habit to pray for the Spirit's help before you read the Bible.

EXPECT GOD TO SPEAK TO YOU

Having prayed for the Spirit's help, it will be natural to expect God to speak through His Word. God speaks not through our hearing His voice in a way audible to our ears but as we become aware that what we read is unmistakably for us. When I'm away from home and my wife writes to me, she speaks to me through what she writes as much as when I hear her voice. I know that what she writes is for me, and it calls forth a response on my part. One of the Puritan writers, Thomas Watson wrote, 'Read the Scriptures, not only as a history, but as a love letter sent you from God, which may affect your heart.' Open your Bible with all the eagerness and expectation with which you open a letter bearing the handwriting of your best friend.

AN IMPORTANT DISTINCTION

Before proceeding to deal with the practicalities of Bible study, we ought to draw a distinction between Bible *reading* and Bible *study*. We shouldn't make too artificial a distinction but there is a difference. I need to read the Bible every day for the benefit of my soul in a time of quiet, when I can also seek God in prayer. For most of us that's first thing in the morning or late at night – or both. Our purpose in brief times of quiet is straightforward Bible reading. Bible study, however, requires more time, and is probably not possible on a daily basis in the same way. Both need to be always linked with prayer, but in our daily times of quiet as much time, if not more, should be given to prayer as to Bible reading. In Bible study, the pattern is reversed.

DAILY BIBLE READING

Daily Bible reading is a 'must'. It's as essential to our soul as eating is to our body. There's no lack of aids for daily Bible reading, and it's important to discover what you find to be the most helpful and to stick with it.

We can read the Bible each day, of course, without the various helps that are published, but the advantage of the aids is that they provide a programme of Bible reading and enable us to do it in fellowship with others. They also supply helpful comment on the passages, although it's important to read the Bible first rather than the comment.

Whatever system of daily Bible reading you follow, I would recommend that it's one that aims to cover the *whole* of the Bible systematically over a period of a few years. '*All* Scripture is God-breathed' (2 Tim. 3:16) and all of it has relevance. Books such as *Daily Light* are excellent supplements to Bible reading, but they are no replacement for it, since they do not cover the whole of Scripture, and they cannot provide the context of the promises and commands that they quote.

If you've never done so before, I would suggest that you aim to write down a verse, or a part of a verse, from each day's reading. Now there will be days when perhaps nothing particularly stands out, but you'll find that most days something does. The benefit of doing this is that it aids and concentrates thought on it – what the Bible calls 'meditation'. Silent reflection on God's Word fixes it in our minds (Ps. 119:15, 48, 97, 148). You'll find that in odd moments of the day, when you've time to think – like the minutes you may spend in a doctor's waiting room – that your mind turns to that key word or verse. It also means that you will have something which is alive and fresh to pass on to others.

BIBLE STUDY

As we turn now to consider Bible study, we have in view those occasions when we can give a longer period of time, probably a minimum of half-an-hour, to study the Bible with a view to enlarging our understanding of it. We won't want to divorce this kind of study from our need to be obedient to the Bible – that would be perilous – but in Bible study we're concerned to understand every part of a passage rather than simply gain strength for the day and a proper stimulus to prayer as we do in Bible reading.

Bible study requires time. It's true that sometimes a few minutes of Bible study may yield immediate fruit, but that's by no means the regular pattern to expect. Some of the most rewarding parts of the Bible need considerable thought and meditation and careful comparison with other Scriptures before they yield up their treasures. If we don't honestly regard Bible study as a priority, we won't have much success, and we'll be forever making fresh starts which are doomed to failure. I've mentioned half-an-hour as a minimum because that's something we can all probably manage once or twice a week. A brief while regularly given to Bible study is more profitable in the end than numerous resolutions to give longer but unrealistic amounts of time to it in the future.

BASIC PRINCIPLES

START WITH THE STRAIGHTFORWARD AND GO ON TO THE MORE DIFFICULT. You may find yourself fascinated and intrigued by the Book of Revelation, but if you've never studied the rest of the Bible in detail the Book of Revelation isn't the place to start. It depends for its symbols and imagery upon the rest of the Bible, and without knowing the rest you'll not only soon find yourself in difficulty, but you'll arrive at wrong conclusions.

Let me suggest an order for studying the Bible, and some of the reasons behind it.

Mark	1 Chronicles	Romans
Genesis	2 Chronicles	Micah
Exodus	Psalms 107–150	Zephaniah
Matthew	1 Timothy	Nahum
Numbers	2 Timothy	Habakkuk
John	Ezra	Leviticus
Deuteronomy	Nehemiah	Hebrews
Joshua	Titus	Jeremiah
Psalm 1-41	Philemon	Lamentations
Luke	Esther	Obadiah
Judges	Job	James
Ruth	Galatians	Ezekiel
1 Samuel	Proverbs	1 Peter
Acts	Philippians	2 Peter
2 Samuel	Ecclesiastes	Haggai
Psalm 42–72	Song of Solomon	1 John
1 Thessalonians	Colossians	2 John
2 Thessalonians	Joel	3 John
1 Kings	Jonah	Zechariah
2 Kings	Amos	Jude
Psalms 73–106	Hosea	Malachi
1 Corinthians	Ephesians	Daniel
2 Corinthians	Isaiah	Revelation

There are important principles behind this suggested order of study. First, it tries to keep a balance between the Old and New Testaments. Second, it endeavours to follow the order either of the Bible itself or the historical order of the books. Mark comes first in the list because it's probably the first gospel to have been written of the four, and it's the shortest and most direct in its teaching. Genesis comes next because it comes first in the Bible's account of the history of things. Where the New Testament letters occur in the list, they begin with 1 and 2 Thessalonians and 1 and 2 Corinthians because they were the earliest parts of the New Testament to be written, even before the gospels. Third, books are put alongside one another where there's obvious profit in considering them together. Judges and Ruth relate to the same period of time, as do Ezra and Nehemiah. Daniel goes well with Revelation because the symbolism and imagery have much in common. Few of us will be able to follow an exact order like this, but it's helpful to have some idea of how we should proceed and what principles should be behind our programme of Bible study.

KNOW THE BACKGROUND OF THE PASSAGES.

Even as our actions can't be understood by an independent observer without his knowing something of our environment, so too many parts of the Bible can't be understood properly without knowledge of the background against which they were set. If we don't appreciate this, we'll often jump to wrong conclusions and even mislead others. The Bible itself provides the historical circumstances we need more often than not, if we'll look for it. It's worthwhile purchasing a one-volume Bible commentary and a one-volume Bible dictionary as soon as we can afford them, since they will both provide introductions to the Bible books we're studying.

WATCH THE CONTEXT.

By 'context' we mean the parts of a chapter or passage which precede and those which follow the part we are considering. Even as the sentence I write now must be understood in relation to the sentence before and the sentence after it, so too all that the Bible says must be understood in relation to the passage in which it is found. To take a verse or a passage out of the Bible without understanding its context may mean that we misunderstand it and then misapply it. (Many of the cults who use the Bible sadly do this.)

USE THE BIBLE TO EXPLAIN THE BIBLE.

Not every part of the Bible is easy to understand when we first read it. Before we reach for the nearest book which will hopefully explain the difficulty, it's worthwhile seeing what other Scriptures have to say on the same subject. If your Bible has references in the centre or at the bottom of its pages they will be helpful. A Bible concordance (a book which lists the Bible's use of words alphabetically) is also invaluable. Then turn to any commentary you have because the author may have thought of parts of the Bible which also deal with the subject which haven't been brought to light by your own looking up of references.

One part of the Bible throws light upon another. Learn to interpret the difficult by means of those passages which are similar and which you already understand. The Bible is invariably its own interpreter if we'll study it patiently. There's much to be said for supplementing our daily Bible reading – which we've already talked about – and our Bible study, with reading the whole of the Bible through with the speed with which we might read any other book and then regularly repeating the process. I've found it helpful to have one copy of the Bible that I keep for this purpose, so that I can mark where I've got up to. Robert Murray M'Cheyne – a famous Scottish minister who died while young after a powerful and influential ministry – provided a calendar for his congregation to enable them to read the whole of the Old Testament once a year and the Book of Psalms and the

New Testament twice. That calendar is still in print and can be purchased cheaply and then used to mark off one's progress. The value of doing this – as an addition to our daily Bible reading of shorter passages – is that almost imperceptibly our knowledge of the whole of the Bible grows, and different Bible truths have a delightful habit of suddenly fitting into their rightful place in our understanding.

METHODS TO USE

Let me suggest briefly some of the more obvious approaches to Bible study and recommend one which will be the most suitable for the majority. First, there are many Bible study books available. Some provide relevant questions to ask when we consider particular Bible books. Such aids are good but the danger is that they may make us lazy, and we can't be dependent for ever upon that sort of book if we're to study the whole of the Bible. The most demanding is the IVP book *Search the Scriptures*, which, if used on a daily basis, covers the whole of the Bible in three years, although it can be spread over a much longer time. But it requires hard work and diligence to complete it.

Second, there are different ways we can approach Bible study on our own. We may divide up a book by its chapters, and then the chapters into paragraphs, giving a descriptive heading to each, to sum up its contents, and then proceed to outline under each paragraph heading the main points of the narrative or argument. It's an ideal way to study the life of a character like Joseph, or to understand a New Testament book which is full of Christian doctrine such as Romans. We may, on the other hand, want to do a Bible study on a subject like guidance or temptation, and for this we'll need a concordance. It's best not to start with topical Bible studies, but to aim to grasp initially the message of complete books.

I would recommend a thorough study first of a gospel, then of a key New Testament letter – like Romans or 1 Peter – followed by an Old Testament book, and the natural place to start is Genesis. It will involve purchasing a good commentary on each of these, but the purchase of commentaries can be staggered over a period of months because you'll only be studying one at a time. Aim so to know the gospel you've chosen to study and the New Testament letter, that you can guide a new Christian through them.

The simplest methods are often the best, and the most straightforward approach to Bible study is what is commonly known as the *Scripture Union* method, because of the questions this Bible Reading organisation encourages readers to ask:

1. What is the main point of this passage?
2. What does it teach about God – the Father, His Son Jesus Christ or the Holy Spirit?
3. Is there a special command, promise, warning, or example that you should note?
4. What fresh insight does the passage give into yourself, your situation and your relationships?
5. What practical action should you take?

We're not meant to find answers to all the questions in every passage we read. But asking these questions will always serve to bring out the main truth which we might well miss if we don't ask such questions.

Once we've become used to this way of approaching a passage we may go on to a more detailed form – providing it proves helpful – and ask 10 questions of a passage:

1. What do the words actually mean?
2. What light do other parts of the Bible throw on this part?
3. Where and how does what this part declares fit into the complete revelation God gives us in the Bible on this subject?

4. What does it teach about God – the Father, the Son and the Holy Spirit?

5. What does it teach about men and women in their relationship to God?

6. What relationship have these words to the saving work of Christ, and what light does the gospel of Christ as a whole throw upon them?

7. What experiences do these words outline, or explain, or try to create or cure?

8. What was the application of these words to the people at the time?

9. How do these words apply to us now?

10. What are we told either to believe or to do?

Do start with the simplest method, and I would suggest the five basic questions of the *Scripture Union*. Don't despise a simple method if it produces results. Some forms of Bible study are much more demanding than others. The most rewarding for you personally will be the one you can cope with on a regular basis and which opens up to you the treasures of God's Word. The most demanding method may not be the most rewarding for you personally. It's a great peril to be over-ambitious and then to become thoroughly disheartened because of failure. Set yourself realistic goals, and plan your week to give an appropriate time for Bible study. With discipline you can do it, and the Holy Spirit is at hand to help you.

There are two practical aspects of Bible study which are so obvious that we may overlook them. First make sure that your Bible for Bible study has large print, so that it is easy to read. A small-print Bible is convenient for carrying around during the day, but it's not ideal for sustained Bible study. Secondly, it's invaluable to write down the fruits of your Bible study in a notebook. The actual writing down of our thoughts serves to encourage clear thinking and also to help us to remember what we've studied. I would also suggest that you use a loose-leaf notebook since it means that you can add to it later, and you will be compiling your own personal commentary which will become increasingly valuable.

Don't neglect the corporate study of the Bible. Part of God's provision to enable us to get to grips with the Bible is the ministry of pastors and teachers. Although I studied theology at university, I've no doubt whatsoever that I learned far more about the Bible through the teaching of God's Word at the local church to which I belonged after I was converted. It may be possible to link your own personal Bible study with the book or subjects that are being taught and studied at church. This will make you all the more attentive in your listening and will enhance your understanding.

When it comes to getting to grips with the Bible the time to start isn't next week or next year, but *now*! Psalm 1 provides a delightful picture of the man who gives God's Word its rightful place.

A Prayer

Father, I cannot praise You sufficiently for Your Word. I thank You that through it I've come to know the truth about You and Your Son and that as living seed it's brought me to new birth through faith in the Lord Jesus.

Make me sensitive to anything that diminishes my appetite for Your Word and quick to seize every opportunity of learning from it. Help me to establish realistic goals and, by the power of Your Spirit, to achieve them. I want never to forget that knowing You is my chief object in my study of the Bible and that Your Son is the key to all that You've revealed in it. Grant that I may be taught, rebuked, corrected and trained in righteousness by

Your Word, so that I may be thoroughly equipped for every good work. I ask this that You may be glorified in my life. For Jesus' sake. Amen.

QUESTIONS

1. How would you answer someone who asked, 'What does the Bible mean to you? What in practice does it do for you?'

2. What are realistic goals to aim at in your Bible reading and Bible study? What practical steps are necessary to fulfil these goals?

BIBLE REFERENCES FOR FURTHER STUDY

THE INSPIRATION AND AUTHORITY OF THE BIBLE:

Exodus 20:1; Joshua 1:7, 8; Psalm 19:7-11; 119:9, 11; Daniel 9:10; Matthew 22:29, 43-45; Luke 24:25-27, 44-48; John 14:26; 15:26, 27; 16:13; 19:24, 28, 36, 37; Acts 17:11; Romans 3:1, 2; 1 Corinthians 15:3, 4; 2 Timothy 3:16, 17; 2 Peter 1:19-21; 3:15.

9

Learn how to pray!

As a Christian, you'll want to pray. That's not to say that prayer is easy, or that you always feel you want to pray. But prayer is an activity that has now become an appropriate daily exercise for you. When Saul – later known as the apostle Paul – was converted, God instructed Ananias, a Christian at Damascus, to go to Saul and lay his hands upon him so that he might recover his sight. To demonstrate that Saul was genuinely converted, God said to Ananias, 'He is praying' (Acts 9:11). New birth is the unique work of God the Holy Spirit, and He is the gift of the Father and the Son to us, and it is He who enables us to cry, '*Abba*, Father' (Rom. 8:15). 'The Spirit himself testifies with our spirit that we are God's children' (Rom. 8:16). One of the many marks of a Christian is that he finds it instinctive to call God 'Father'.

'OUR FATHER'

As a general rule we should address our prayers to God the Father. It's not inappropriate to direct our prayers to God the Son and to God the Holy Spirit, but that is not the pattern we find in the Bible, and for obvious reasons. The initiative in the whole scheme of redemption was God the Father's (cf. John 3:16; 1 John 3:1; 4:14), and one of the great objectives of the plan of salvation is that through the Lord Jesus we should 'have access to the Father by one Spirit' (Eph. 2:18). As it's often been expressed, the Lord Jesus the Son of God became the Son of Man that we might become the sons and daughters of God; and as such we delight to call God 'Father'. In the Lord's Prayer we're taught to begin our prayers with the words, 'Our Father' (Matt. 6:9).

LEARN TO PRAY BY PRAYING AND HEARING OTHERS PRAY

The picture of a young child, which the analogy of adoption suggests, is helpful. As young children develop, it's instinctive for them to learn to talk. At first they may be faltering and disjointed in what they say, but the more they endeavour to express themselves the more proficient they become. In a similar way, we learn to pray by praying. If we don't pray, we won't learn to pray. As parents delight in the first words of their son or daughter, so God delights in our first words to Him. While words are important, and we naturally want to express ourselves correctly, we must never forget that God always looks beyond our words to our hearts, and He's not limited by the way we express ourselves, even when we are at our clumsiest.

We learn to pray by hearing others pray. This is an aspect of prayer sometimes overlooked. Young children develop their capacity for speech by listening to the conversations of their parents and any other members of the family. I'm grateful that within days of my professing faith as a Christian I was encouraged to go to a church prayer meeting. It was through listening to the prayers of others and adding my 'Amen' to them, that I unconsciously received my first lessons in prayer. Aim to join together with other Christians to pray, and if someone was especially instrumental in your conversion, it might be helpful meeting with that person to share a prayer time together.

DISCOVER THE FULLNESS OF PRAYER

Discovering the richness of prayer is a great adventure. Many descriptions of prayer are found in the Bible, and we'll pick out a few which hopefully summarise most of them. Prayer is *asking God*. Sometimes this fact is stated with a sense of apology, but that should not be the case. Of course, prayer is much more than just asking God for things; but, nevertheless, it has asking at its very heart. 'Ask and it will be given to you' the Lord Jesus said, 'seek and you will find; knock and the door will be opened to you. For everyone who asks receives; he who seeks finds; and to him who knocks, the door will be opened' (Matt. 7:7, 8). Remembering that God is now our Heavenly Father, it's not at all surprising that He's willing to give good gifts to His children (Matt. 7:11). Any human father who loves his children delights to give them gifts – he's glad that he has the privilege of being uniquely responsible for them. Our Heavenly Father loves us to express our dependence upon Him and to look to Him as to no one else for the supply of our needs.

Prayer is *the offering up of our desires to God*. When we were children we learnt a lot about our father's wishes by asking him for things and by telling him what we wanted. Often he would say 'No', and it was by the things that he said 'Yes' to, and the things he said 'No' to, that we discovered not only what pleased him but what was best for us. Likewise in prayer, God encourages us to bring *all* our desires and wishes before Him, for by so doing we discover what pleases Him and what's best for us. If the desire isn't granted then we know that God's answer is 'No'.

Prayer is *the surrendering of our wills to God*. The more we know God our Heavenly Father, through His Son our Lord Jesus Christ, the more assured we become of His love and the perfection of His plan for our life. Aware too of God's mercy in saving us and bringing us into His kingdom, we'll want to live with the sole aim of pleasing Him. It's in prayer that such longings are best expressed, and it's there too that we seek to make our will coincide with God's will.

The Lord Jesus never suggested that following Him would lead to an easy life without difficulties. In fact, the opposite is what He taught. Obedience to God's will may sometimes be costly, and we'll be tempted to shrink from doing what we know God wants. We'll often feel the need to pray through difficult situations on our knees. None delighted to do the Father's will more than our Lord Jesus Christ, but He knew tremendous inner conflict as He viewed the prospect of the cross. Honestly He poured out His desires to His Father, and three times He asked, 'My Father, if it is possible, may this cup be taken from me', but at the same time He prayed, 'Yet not as I will, but as you will' (Matt. 26:39).

When there's a battle involved in bringing our wills into submission to God, prayer is the means of winning the battle. We'll often find, as our Lord did, that we will need to repeat our prayer of submission a number of times to arrive honestly at the point where we do choose God's will in preference to our own.

A very practical way of surrendering our wills to God's will in prayer is to link it with our daily Bible reading. Always make a point of checking that what you read concerning God's will in the Bible is actually being done in your life. There are few occasions that I read the Bible when it doesn't direct me into God's will, and if I respond by praying home what I read I'll be keeping my life in His will. If someone asked me, 'How do you know that your watch is telling the right time?' I'd probably answer that every time I hear the pips on the radio preceding the news or the chimes of Big Ben I instinctively look at my watch. I never doubt that the pips or the chimes are right, and I'm always open to the possibility of my watch being wrong and needing adjustment. Our lives are like watches when they are exposed to God's Word, and it's by prayer that we put them right, surrendering ourselves afresh to His will.

Prayer is *being with God*. God's presence is difficult to define, but it's a benefit of which we become aware. We are never closer to God than when we come to Him in the name of His dear Son. There will be times when we feel particularly needy, perhaps even desperate, and yet we won't know exactly what's wrong or what we should say. The most secure place for us then is God's presence. No matter how busy I was when our children were young, I never resented the little head that might poke itself around my study door, and say, 'Daddy, may I be with you?' I felt privileged that I represented a form of security to my children. Our heavenly Father delights in our seeking Him simply for His own sake, just because we want to be near Him. Sometimes we may be so overwhelmed by sorrow or depression, that all we can cry is 'Father!' but that's enough to bring us into God's presence and for Him to show His love to us.

Prayer is *conversation with God*. I wouldn't want to exaggerate this aspect of prayer, but it would be a mistake to overlook it. As we read the Scriptures, God speaks. It's not that we hear His voice – as we might hear a human voice – but we become aware of His Spirit applying what we read to our heart and conscience. We know that what's written is for us, and we see how it applies to us in a way it might not apply to others. Then in prayer we reply to God. As He reveals His love, we respond in thanksgiving and tell Him that we love Him. As He shows us what we should do – and it may be something as practical as making an apology to someone – we tell Him that we'll do it, and we'll ask Him for strength to make the apology graciously and genuinely.

There's obvious value in silence in prayer, in moments when we think over situations in God's presence, and ponder the application of the principles of His Word to our immediate circumstances. Increasingly we'll come to recognise the still, small voice of His Spirit saying, 'This is the way; walk in it' (Isa. 30:21), and we'll respond, 'Your will be done, Lord.'

Prayer is *the way to peace*. God is the God of peace, and as our Heavenly Father He wants us to enjoy His peace. Prayer would be impossible without the glorious truth that we have peace with God through our Lord Jesus Christ (Rom. 5:1, 2), and as a result we are in a position to enjoy God's peace in our lives.

The route to peace is prayer, and the Bible speaks plainly about this. Paul wrote, 'Do not be anxious about anything, but in everything, by prayer and petition, with thanksgiving, present your requests to God. And the peace of God, which transcends all understanding, will guard your hearts and your minds in Christ Jesus' (Phil. 4:6, 7). Peter urges, 'Cast all your anxiety on him because he cares for you' (1 Pet. 5:7). Our temperaments vary, and some of us worry more than others. But whatever our temperament prayer remains God's solution to our anxieties. It's little things that frequently bother us – often issues that we would be too ashamed to admit to others as matters of concern. God wants us to pray about these very things – about *anything*. Whatever bothers me matters to God, and therefore should be the subject of my prayers. God's peace is always available to us, but prayer is our part in obtaining it.

EXPLORE THE CONSTITUENT PARTS OF PRAYER

Paul's encouraging words to the Philippians about prayer (4:6, 7) mention prayer, petition and thanksgiving – and there are other parts to prayer too. It's good to explore them so that our relationship to God in prayer deepens and our knowledge of Him grows.

The place to begin is *adoration*. In adoration we recognise who and what God is, and we endeavour to express our appreciation and, in particular, our reverence of Him. We remember that 'He is more awesome than all who surround him' (Ps. 89:7). We bow in spirit before Him and worship. Adoration is helped as we deliberately meditate on the different aspects of God's character. I've found it helpful to make a list of the truths I know about God and then to meditate upon one of them each day as I begin to pray.

Hard on the heels of adoration comes *praise*. As we contemplate God's greatness and glory, we find ourselves declaring, 'I call to the Lord, who is worthy of praise' (Ps. 18:3). By praise we give God glory for what He is in Himself. We don't find praise difficult if we deliberately meditate upon God's character and all that we know of Him through our Lord Jesus Christ. As a Creole-speaking Jamaican granny put it, 'Me cannot find tongue, Missus, to praise His Name!' Archbishop Leighton wrote many years ago, 'What are our lame praises in comparison of His love? Nothing, and less than nothing; but love will stammer rather than be dumb'.

Next comes *thanksgiving* in which we recall what God has done. In thanksgiving we review God's dealings with us and the material and spiritual benefits He's poured out upon us. And we won't be able to do so without exclaiming, 'The Lord has done great things for us, and we are filled with joy' (Ps. 126:3). Casting our minds over our spiritual blessings in Christ, we'll exclaim, 'Praise be to the God and Father of our Lord Jesus Christ!' (Eph. 1:3).

Thanksgiving is a most necessary part of prayer because God consistently answers our prayers, and so there's always room for looking back and recognising God's answers. On His way to Jerusalem the Lord Jesus healed ten men who had leprosy. 'One of them, when he saw he was healed, came back, praising God in a loud voice. He threw himself at Jesus' feet and thanked him – and he was a Samaritan. Jesus asked, "Were not all ten cleansed?

Where are the other nine?"'(Luke 17:15-17). In thanksgiving we avoid the mistake and ingratitude of the nine and follow the example of the one. Thanksgiving is a great stimulus to prayer because it causes us to recall how God has answered our prayers on previous occasions when we've committed to Him matters which have caused us great anxiety.

Confession of our sins must have a regular place in our prayers. Adoring God, we think of His holiness, and that shows up our sinfulness afresh. As we praise Him for His constancy, we become conscious of our own lack of consistency and faithfulness. Thanking Him, we so often recall our frequent ingratitude and sometimes unbelief. Reading the Bible, we'll be made aware of how we've fallen short of God's will and good purposes.

Our awareness of our sins isn't meant to drive us to despair — rather it's meant to lead us to confess them so that we may find fresh cleansing and restoration of our fellowship with God. It's good to remember that had we not been converted and born again, we wouldn't have the awareness we presently possess of our sinfulness. It's because we are now striving to live our lives in fellowship with God, who is Light, that we've become sensitive to so many dark areas in our lives.

Confession of sin needs to be specific rather than general, where possible. In other words, it's not enough to say, 'Lord, forgive me my *sin* ...' but rather I need to confess my actual *sins*. So I might have to confess, 'Lord, I've been jealous ... or envious ... please forgive me.' The Bible's promise of forgiveness emphasises this aspect of confession: 'If we confess our *sins*, he is faithful and just and will forgive us our *sins* and purify us from all unrighteousness' (1 John 1:9). To actually name my sins as I confess them to God in prayer is a necessary part of honesty before Him, and nothing serves to make me hate the sins I confess more than having to be specific about them.

Prayer, supplication and intercession are aspects of what asking God in prayer includes. The distinction between prayer and supplication is helpful. By *prayer* the Bible has in mind those general requests we feel bound to make regularly to God – such as praying for the leaders of our nation and the provision of our daily bread. By *supplication* the Bible has in view specific requests for immediate situations. While we pray in a general manner for the well-being of our nation, when a crisis arises we will make special supplication for God's intervention or for His wisdom to be given. Similarly, while we pray regularly 'Give us today our daily bread', when times of material and financial difficulty come, we'll offer urgent supplication to God to meet our immediate need. Our praying should be a constant mixture of praying for general needs that are always present and specific situations which are urgent and require God's immediate intervention.

In *intercession* we approach God on behalf of others. Many a time we may feel unworthy to ask God anything for ourselves, but we'll feel duty bound to pray for other people, feeling as Samuel did about the Israelites, 'Far be it from me that I should sin against the Lord by failing to pray for you' (1 Sam. 12:23). To be effective in intercession involves effort. An important key is trying to put ourselves in the place of the person for whom we are praying. The writer to the Hebrews puts it so well when he writes, 'Remember those in prison as if you were their fellow-prisoners, and those who are ill-treated as if you yourselves were suffering' (Heb. 13:3). As you pray for a missionary, think yourself first into his or her position, perhaps struggling with a difficult language and an oppressive climate. As you remember a friend in hospital, try to imagine what goes through his mind, and pray accordingly. I find it helpful to pray for others in the light of what I've prayed for myself after having read the Scriptures that day, and this helps to keep prayer fresh and different.

Dedication is also an aspect of prayer, hinted at in our description of prayer as a means of surrendering our wills to God. As we lay each day before Him, we want Him to prepare us in soul and mind for obedience to His will, and we should tell Him so and give ourselves afresh to Him (Rom. 12:1, 2). In reading the biography of Cyril Garbett, a former Archbishop of York, I was challenged by a daily prayer of self-dedication which he used: 'Lord, I am Thy servant, utterly unworthy, but in Thy love use me: shine through me: I give myself to Thee'. In the back of my Bible I've pasted the prayer of King Henry VI, 'O Lord Jesus Christ, who hast created and redeemed me, and hast brought me unto that which now I am; Thou knowest what Thou wouldest do with me: do with me according to Thy will, for Thy tender mercy's sake. Amen'.

While I've put these different parts of prayer into something of a logical order, it's not to suggest that we should slavishly follow it. Circumstances may dictate otherwise. I may find myself in an emergency situation in which as soon as I begin to pray, the urgent crisis is uppermost in my mind, and that's what God would have me pray for without delay. On the other hand, I may be overwhelmed by my sense of sin, so that I don't feel in a proper position to adore and praise God, and, in the words of John Newton's hymn, I have to pray:

> With my burden I begin:
> Lord, remove this load of sin;
> Let Thy blood, for sinners spilt,
> Set my conscience free from guilt.

Let the logical order of the different parts of prayer be a helpful guide but not a hard and fast rule.

BE GUIDED BY THE PRAYERS FOUND IN THE BIBLE

Learning by example is an excellent form of instruction, and we can't do better than be guided by the examples of prayer the

Bible itself contains. The obvious starting point is what we know as the Lord's Prayer, a prayer our Lord Jesus gave His disciples when they came to Him with the request, 'Lord, teach us to pray, just as John taught his disciples' (Luke 11:1). It's a prayer which we ourselves may pray with profit, both together with other Christians and on our own. But in particular it provides a spiritual agenda for prayer, in that it teaches us to pray for six things: the honour of God's Name in the world; the extension of the church and the coming of God's kingdom through the preaching of the gospel; the obedience of God's people to His will and God's overruling control of all the events of the world; our daily practical needs and our work; our relationships, both with God and others, and their maintenance through the experience of forgiveness; and our temptations and the spiritual battle in which all Christians are involved. Those six headings are amazingly comprehensive.

Paul's prayers in the New Testament are rich in content and example, and are worthy not only of study but of actual use (we'll list some of them at the end of the chapter). The Book of Psalms, besides being a song book, is also a prayer book. Weighed down by sin, you'll find guidance and relief in praying the words of Psalm 51. Overwhelmed by depression, you'll find appropriate words to use in Psalms 42 and 43.

INTRODUCE AN ELEMENT OF ORGANISATION AND METHOD INTO YOUR PRAYING

The Lord's Prayer is a most orderly prayer, beginning with a concern for God's Name, kingdom and will and then turning to the needs we have as individuals. Paul's prayers indicate that he must have had some method to cope with praying regularly for so many people. In such a busy life, he must have been self-disciplined to give so much time to prayer. We know from the gospels that our Lord Jesus Christ got up early, before daybreak, in order to be alone with His Father (Mark 1:35).

Discipline is essential for prayer. While we can pray at any time and anywhere, we need to establish when we should have our main time or times of prayer each day. No matter how difficult to achieve, there's much to be said for the beginning of the day. But early rising can't be sustained without avoiding late nights. In the evening may be the best time for you, but ensure that you don't leave it so late that you're too tired to give of your best to God. A friend of mine used to get into his office half-an-hour before anyone else each morning so that he could have that time alone with God. We all need to establish what is best for us, and then to aim at it consistently. Sometimes praying at the same spot – perhaps kneeling at the same chair – helps because we are naturally creatures of habit, and hopefully of good habits! If you find concentration difficult, I would suggest that you pray aloud if you've a room to yourself. I often walk as I pray because I've discovered that it helps my concentration, especially if I'm tired, and to kneel could sometimes soon find me asleep!

The most useful practical asset in the organisation of prayer is a prayer diary. It's a most personal aid to produce, and I wouldn't want to suggest that you do exactly as I do, but it's worth thinking of what would be most appropriate and helpful for you. On my first page I list urgent matters as they arise which need to be remembered before God daily. Then I have seven pages – one for each day of the week – for people and subjects of concern that I want to pray for once a week. After that there follow 31 pages – a page for each day of an average month – in which I space out the many people I've come to know over the years for whom I feel I have a responsibility in prayer. To the various pages of my prayer diary I've added – and still add – verses of Scripture which help me to focus on God or on His purposes for my life.

They often provide my starting point for either adoration of God or meditation. I would recommend using a small loose-leaf notebook so that you can add and remove pages without having to rewrite the whole diary.

DEPEND ON YOUR CHIEF HELPER

Any good thing we do regularly can become meaningless routine if we're not careful – and prayer isn't immune from that danger. If ever you feel that you're getting into a rut following a particular method in your praying, change it for a day. I will often not use my prayer diary one day a week simply to avoid getting into the position where I feel ruled by it. Instead I'll engage in prayer following some other order.

Whatever happens don't allow your moods to dictate whether or not you pray. It's great to feel we want to pray and that we're getting through to God. But to pray only on such occasions is a mistake. Our Lord taught that we 'should always pray and not give up' (Luke 18:1). The moments when we don't feel like praying – often for a variety of reasons, and some unknown – are frequently the occasions when we most need to pray.

Whenever you feel you're getting into a rut or that prayer is difficult, immediately ask God for the help of the Holy Spirit. An essential part of God's purpose in giving us His Spirit is that He should assist us in our praying: 'The Spirit helps us in our weakness. We do not know what we ought to pray for, but the Spirit himself intercedes for us with groans that words cannot express. And he who searches our hearts knows the mind of the Spirit, because the Spirit intercedes for the saints in accordance with God's will' (Rom. 8:26, 27).

No one knows better than God the help we cry out for, and in His gift of the Spirit He's provided Someone who's able to meet perfectly the needs we have, and not least support in prayer. While our Lord Jesus is our Advocate with the Father and appears in God's presence on our behalf, the Holy Spirit is our Advocate in another sense in that He puts pleas and words into our mouths as we pray which are acceptable to our Father as we pray in Jesus' Name. It's the Holy Spirit who prompts us to pray for the right things as He places a burden upon us (Rom. 9:1, 2; 10:1), or brings people to mind in the course of a day.

One of the most foolish things we can do is to grieve the Holy Spirit, for then we limit the assistance He gives us. As a boy, John Laing, the well-known builder, often got into trouble at school, and he learnt a lesson which was to remain with him throughout his Christian life. The headmaster, Mr Crossthwaite, came into the classroom during the form-master's absence and found a free fight going on. John Laing panicked. 'His only way out was to tell a lie, and he told it. That night he found that he could not pray. His conscience taunted him: "You are a hypocrite." He told himself: "Oh, this will soon wear off." But after a fortnight it had not worn off. In desperation, he thought: "Is that lie going to be allowed to spoil my whole life?" Still he had not the courage to tell Mr Crossthwaite; but he wrote a note of confession and put it on the Head's desk. That evening he found he could pray.' When prayer is difficult, always be prepared to ask God, 'Have I grieved Your Holy Spirit?' If God doesn't then give you an awareness of sin to be confessed, cry to Him for the Spirit's help and pray!

NEVER LOSE THE SENSE OF WONDER THAT SHOULD ACCOMPANY PRAYER

It's almost incredible that you and I - frail, limited, finite creatures – can enjoy the fellowship of God who is almighty and infinite, and yet that's our privilege. We 'who once were far away have been brought near through the blood of Christ' (Eph. 2:13).

Every prayer we offer rests upon the finished work of our Lord Jesus Christ on the cross. It's in the Lord Jesus' Name that we pray because it's in His Name that we are accepted by God. Our times of prayer do not need to be limited to the first part of the day or the end. Wherever we are, we can call upon God and know that He hears and answers our cry. It's through prayer that we learn to enjoy God's intimate friendship.

A PRAYER

Father, first I want to thank You that I may call You 'Father' and know that is what You really are to me. I know that I wouldn't be able to do this apart from Your Son's death upon the cross, by which He dealt once and for all with the problem of my sin. I thank You too for the gift of Your Holy Spirit to live in me and how He enables me to cry 'Abba, Father!'

Please teach me how to pray. Where there's a need for greater discipline in prayer, I seek Your guidance. Please make prayer mean to me all that You intend it should. May I never lose its wonder, and through it may I enjoy intimate friendship with You and Your Son, Jesus Christ, in whose Name I pray. Amen.

QUESTIONS

1. What times in the day do you find it best to pray, and why?
2. How do you organise your times of prayer? Do you feel you have sufficient method in prayer? In what areas of prayer do you feel you should be growing?

BIBLE REFERENCES FOR FURTHER STUDY
Various Bible passages which describe prayer:

AN ACTIVITY OF THE SOUL
Luke 1:46, 47

AN EXPRESSION OF GOD'S INTIMATE FRIENDSHIP
Job 29:4

POURING OUT OUR HEARTS TO GOD
Psalm 62:8; Lamentations 2:19; 1 Samuel 1:15, 16

COMMUNING WITH GOD
1 John 1:3; 2 Corinthians 12:7-9

ACCESS TO GOD
James 4:8; Romans 5:1, 2; Hebrews 10:19; 1 John 5:14

APPROACHING THE THRONE OF GRACE
Hebrews 4:16

LOOKING TO GOD
Ezra 8:22; Psalm 34:5

CALLING ON GOD'S NAME
1 Kings 18:24

SEEKING GOD
Psalm 34:10

SEEKING GOD'S FACE
Psalm 27:8

ASKING
Matthew 7:7, 8; Philippians 4:6

SOME OF PAUL'S PRAYERS:
Romans 15:5, 6, 13; Ephesians 1:15-23; 3:14-21;
Philippians 1:9-11; Colossians 1:9-12; 1 Thessalonians 3:11-13;
5:23; 2 Thessalonians 2:16, 17; 3:5.

10

Get your focus right!

What's the secret of success in the Christian life? That's a necessary question to ask if we're concerned to grow 'in the grace and knowledge of our Lord and Saviour Jesus Christ' (2 Pet. 3:18). All the many answers that might be given add up to this: get your focus right.

One winter a teacher in a Canadian school asked the children in her class to compete against one another in trying to walk in a straight line in the snow. They thought this was an easy assignment, but they soon discovered otherwise. As they looked back, they saw that their tracks were far from straight. One boy's path in the snow, however, was absolutely straight, in sharp distinction from the others. The children crowded around, and the teacher asked, 'What's your secret?' 'Well,' replied the boy, 'I didn't look down at my feet. Do you see that tall tree over there? I kept my eyes fixed on the tree all the time, and that kept me walking in a straight line.' His skill in keeping a straight course was not focusing on his feet but upon the tree.

FIX YOUR THOUGHTS ON JESUS

We get everything into proper focus as we see the Lord Jesus as central to everything. It's as we fix our eyes firmly on Him that our feet are kept walking in the right direction, without harmful deviations. It seems such an obvious principle, but it's easily neglected, and not least because the enemy of our souls knows how important the principle is and constantly endeavours to sidetrack us from it.

The writer to the Hebrews has this matter of focus as a primary emphasis in his letter. 'Fix your thoughts on Jesus,' he urges. 'Let us fix our eyes on Jesus, the author and finisher of our faith … Consider him …' (Heb. 3:1; 12:2, 3). There must be nothing casual or haphazard about our fixing our thoughts on the Lord Jesus Christ. We are to do it carefully, giving time to reflecting on who He is, what He has done for us and all that He is to us. We won't achieve this goal without deliberate effort, because it involves turning our eyes away from other things or people that might distract us. We must firmly establish in our minds that the Lord Jesus Christ Himself is to be our supreme preoccupation – and this is exactly what the Bible encourages.

THE CENTRE OF ALL GOD'S PURPOSES

The great secret the Bible reveals – sometimes called the 'mystery' – is that the Lord Jesus Christ is the unrivalled centre of all God's purposes. All the blessings of God, for example, that come to us are blessings 'in Christ' (Eph. 1:3ff). 'No matter how many promises God has made, they are "Yes" in Christ. And so through him the "Amen" is spoken by us to the glory of God' (2 Cor. 1:20). The Holy Spirit, the gift of the Father and the Son to every Christian, is *the Spirit of Christ* (1 Pet. 1:11; Rom. 8:9; Phil. 1:19), and one of the reasons for this description is His supreme objective of speaking not about Himself but about the Lord Jesus. Explaining the work of the Holy Spirit, the Lord Jesus said, 'He will bring glory to me by taking from what is mine and making it known to you. All that belongs to the Father is mine. That is why I said the Spirit will take from what is mine and make it known to you' (John 16:14, 15).

God's purpose is that in everything the Lord Jesus might be pre-eminent (Col. 1:18). Jesus Christ our Lord must have first place in all things – that is God's declared purpose and will. It implies the consequent secondary status of other people and things. In a variety of ways, over the centuries, Christians have been tempted to lose sight in their thinking of the central place of the Lord Jesus.

Two New Testament letters – Colossians and Hebrews – were written with the primary aim of establishing in a Christian's mind the unrivalled central place the Lord Jesus has in God's purposes and the unique position He must have in a Christian's life. Hebrews, for example, sets out the Lord Jesus Christ's superiority to the angels, to Aaron and Moses and to all who had been before Him, and declares Him to be the one set over the whole household of faith (Heb. 3:6). Colossians demonstrates that the Lord Jesus has first place because He is the unique image of God, the first-born of all creation and the One through whom all things were created, and now hold together (Col. 1:15-17). He and no one else is the Head of the church, His body, and in Him all the fullness of God was pleased to dwell (Col. 1:19), and through Him alone has God reconciled to Himself all things whether on earth or in heaven, making peace by the blood of the Lord Jesus' cross (Col. 1:20). Well may we sing:

> *There's no greater name than Jesus,*
> *name of Him who came to save us;*
> *in that saving name so gracious*
> *every knee shall bow.*

Let everything that's beneath the ground,
let everything in the world around,
let everything exalted on high
bow at Jesus' name!
In our minds, by faith professing,
in our hearts, by inward blessing,
on our tongues, by words confessing,
Jesus Christ is Lord. (Michael Baughen)

We sing such words because they are the truth (Phil. 2:9-11)!

THE OBJECT OF OUR FAITH

From beginning to end the Christian life is a life of faith –
we've established that fact already. The supreme object of our
faith is Jesus Christ Himself. That in no way detracts from our
faith in God the Father. Explaining how his readers had become
Christians, Peter writes, 'Through him (Jesus) you believe in
God, who raised him from the dead and glorified him, and so
your faith and hope are in God' (1 Pet. 1:21). The Lord Jesus is
the way, the truth and the life, the One through whom we alone
may come to the Father (John 14:6). God has chosen to make
Himself known to us supremely in the Person of His dear Son,
so that our faith should be in His Son, the exact representation
of His Being (Heb. 1:3), for in trusting Him we trust the Father
who has given Him to us.

Healthy faith grows: it doesn't remain static. Static faith
decreases in power. Our faith first came to birth as the Holy
Spirit revealed the Lord Jesus to us, and our faith continues
to grow as we discover more of Him. The more we know
Him, the more trustworthy we know Him to be – and thus
faith grows. But our part is to fix our gaze on the Lord Jesus.
The secret of faith is not saying to myself, 'I must have greater
faith' but rather appreciating how great and glorious Jesus
Christ is.

One of the most enriching experiences of my life, in terms of the help that has come through books, was my reading of Hudson Taylor's biography. Hudson Taylor, the founder of the China Inland Mission (now OMF International), had reached a critical point in the growth of his faith, and he received a letter which helped him immeasurably; and a quotation from it in his biography benefited me. Hudson Taylor wrote, 'The part especially helpful to me is: "How then to have our faith increased? Only by thinking of all that Jesus *is*, and all He is *for us*: His life, His death, His work, He Himself as revealed to us in the Word, to be the subject of our constant thoughts. *Not* a striving to have faith, to increase our faith, *but* a looking off to the Faithful One seems *all* we need."'

One Sunday in our morning service we had been considering an aspect of the Lord Jesus Christ's Person and work. The service had ended, and everyone had gone home, and I was the last person to leave. As I was about to shut the door of the church, a young fellow called Tony came cycling back. 'Have you left something behind, Tony?' I asked. 'No,' he said, 'I just wanted to come back and say, isn't the Lord wonderful!' When we are understanding that, our faith grows strong. But it requires our focusing upon Jesus. As the Lord Jesus is the object of our focus, other priorities fall into place.

THE RIGHT EXAMPLE

No one would doubt that the proper way to live the Christian life is to follow the example of the Lord Jesus Christ in every way possible. As Christians we are 'followers' of Jesus Christ. We are meant to live as He lived. With His Spirit living within us, we possess a new dynamic and power to enable us to follow our Lord's example. But the key to achieving this aim is to focus on Him so that we have His example constantly before us.

The New Testament regularly points to Jesus' example and calls us to follow it. He set us an example that we should follow in His steps (1 Pet. 2:21). First and foremost, He is the perfect example of obedience to God's will. When He came into the world, He said to His Father, 'Here I am ... I have come to do your will, O God' (Heb. 10:7). 'My food,' He said, 'is to do the will of him who sent me and to finish his work' (John 4:34). With the agony of the cross before Him, He prayed in the Garden of Gethsemane, 'My Father, if it is possible, may this cup be taken from me. Yet not as I will, but as you will' (Matt. 26:39). That's the kind of obedience God wants.

Our Lord Jesus Christ's love is an example of the love we are to show one another. 'A new command I give you,' He says to us, 'Love one another. As I have loved you, so you must love one another' (John 13:34). We are to 'live a life of love, just as Christ loved us and gave Himself up for us as a fragrant offering and sacrifice to God' (Eph. 5:2). This is a very practical love. It means we are to forgive one another as He has forgiven us (Col. 3:13), and to accept one another as He has accepted us (Rom. 15:7).

Let's be honest. It's not easy to love everyone. We may find ourselves very different in character and personality from another Christian. Perhaps he's done us some wrong, or he's not the kind of person we would naturally choose as a friend. If we react as normal human beings, we'll show those feelings and throw up invisible barriers. But what happens when we fix our eyes on Jesus and His example? We find our attitudes have to change. He loved us – and loves us still – when our characters and personalities are far from what they ought to be. He's forgiven us *all* our sins and welcomed us. With our eyes upon Him, we can do nothing other than the same to others.

The Lord Jesus is our example of humility (Phil. 2:5ff). Humility doesn't come easily to any of us. It's essentially something we have to do rather than simply pray for. In practical terms it means determining to do nothing out of selfish ambition or pride. It requires that we genuinely consider others better than ourselves and strive to see things from other people's point of view. In pursuing it we may make ourselves extremely vulnerable since others may take advantage of our humility. Left to myself I'm naturally inclined to think of my rights, but if in my mind's eye I have the picture of the Lord Jesus washing the disciples' feet, I know that the only proper course of action is to be willing to do the most menial task for others if I can do it in His Name (John 13:1-17). As He was among men and women as one who served, so must I be (Luke 22:27). 'He went around doing good' (Acts 10:38), and that must be the pattern for my life too (Matt. 5:16).

At no time is it more important to fix our eyes upon the Lord Jesus than when we are unjustly treated. Peter reminds us that 'When they hurled their insults at him, he did not retaliate; when he suffered, he made no threats. Instead, he entrusted himself to him who judges justly' (1 Pet. 2:23) – and in this He set us an example that we should follow in His footsteps (1 Pet. 2:21). We can't escape being misunderstood sometimes or unjustly treated. The natural inclination is to want to justify ourselves and to see that justice is done. But so often the desire for personal redress aggravates the situation, causes bad feeling and mars human relationships. It's important to distinguish between sticking up for oneself and sticking up for the interests of others. The Lord Jesus stood up for others, but when He Himself was ill-treated, He remained silent and allowed His Father to be His vindicator.

We may have wondered sometimes, 'Why is it that Christians are so often unlike the Lord Jesus Christ?' The answer must be, in part at least, that they fail to focus upon the Lord Jesus and His example. The idea behind Peter's use of the word 'example'

(1 Pet. 2:21) is the way children were taught to write. On one line the teacher wrote in perfect handwriting the letters of the alphabet or some sentences, and on the line below the child copied exactly – to the best of his ability – what was above the line. Without his eye upon the line above, the child couldn't reproduce on the line below what was written above. If we take our eyes off Jesus, we'll fail to reproduce His example; with our eyes on Him, we're more than halfway to achieving the goal.

ACCELERATING THE PROCESS OF CHANGE

Tied in with the key importance of Jesus' example is the Bible's assurance that the secret of our transformation in character to the likeness of Jesus Christ is our reflecting His glory (2 Cor. 3:18). God's declared purpose is to set us apart to become like His Son (Rom. 8:29). The Lord Jesus, God's only Son, is the supreme object of the Father's delight, and nothing pleases Him more than to see His Son's character reproduced and reflected in us. Holiness becomes our happy objective when we fix our eyes on Jesus.

LOVE AND JOY

One of my favourite verses in Peter's first letter is found in chapter one, verse eight: 'Though you have not seen him, you love him; and even though you do not see him now, you believe in him and are filled with an inexpressible and glorious joy'. When we love someone, we regularly think of that person, and the more we think of him or her the more our love grows. If we go away from home, we probably take a photo to stir up our memory and to quicken our love. When our love is reciprocated, we have tremendous joy. And so it is in our relationship with the Lord Jesus. Loving Him, we think a lot about Him. As we recall His love, it fills us with joy and stirs us up to love Him and thus to think of Him even more – and so the marvellous process of growing love and joy goes on.

One of the purposes of the Lord's Supper – and why we should take every opportunity of joining in its celebration – is to remind us of our Lord's amazing love and to focus our thoughts on His cross as we recall how He gave Himself for us. The obedience to which the Lord Jesus calls us is never difficult when we love Him. One of the most attractive features of Christian testimony is the surprising joy Christians can exhibit no matter how tough life may be.

THE SECRET OF PERSEVERANCE

The real test of a person's reality as a Christian is his perseverance. The Lord Jesus explained that it is the person who continues to the end who will be saved (Matt. 10:22). We have complete confidence that when God begins a good work in our life He will finish it (Phil. 1:6). But the secret of perseverance is focusing our attention on the Lord Jesus. The writer of Hebrews sums up Moses' experience like this: 'He persevered because he saw him who is invisible' (Heb. 11:27). That paradoxical statement makes sense to the Christian. He's never seen the Lord Jesus with his physical eyes, but he knows what it is to see Him with the eyes of his faith, with the eyes of his soul.

We'll have to take many knocks in life. Being a Christian doesn't exempt us from pain, suffering, difficulty and bereavement. Faith itself will be sorely tested, and Satan, the tempter, will have the audacity to suggest that God doesn't exist and that all our Christian commitment is in vain. But, by the help of the Holy Spirit, we'll be able to use our invisible weapon of spiritual focus. Stephen, the first Christian martyr, whose story is described in Acts 7, found himself under tremendous pressure. Besides being opposed by his own people he was about to be stoned to death. Luke, the writer of Acts, tells us, 'But Stephen, full of the Holy Spirit, looked up to heaven and saw the glory of God, and Jesus standing at the right hand of God. "Look," he said, "I see heaven open and the Son of Man standing at the right hand of God" ' (Acts 7:55, 56). It wasn't with his physical eyes that he saw Jesus, but filled with the Spirit he saw Him with the eyes of his soul. That spiritual focus enabled him to follow Jesus' example, so that he could even pray, 'Lord, do not hold this sin against them' (Acts 7:60), after the pattern of Jesus' own example upon the cross (Luke 23:34).

Stephen wasn't the first to discover this secret of spiritual focus, since David and many others in the Old Testament knew it too. David wrote, 'My eyes are ever on the Lord, for only he will release my feet from the snare ...Those who look to him are radiant; their faces are never covered with shame' (Ps. 25:15; 34:5). To focus our gaze upon the Lord Jesus in times of trouble is the best antidote to the poison there may be in them. It's an incredible truth of Christian experience that in times of greatest difficulty our despondency can be exchanged for actual radiance as we turn our eyes away from the troubles to the Lord Jesus and then look at them in the light of His grace and power.

OUR GLORIOUS FUTURE

If fixing our eyes on the Lord Jesus fires our love for Him, it also makes us want to see Him and to be with Him. It brings into proper focus the future aspect of our salvation. The Lord Jesus Himself is our Hope for the future, and by 'hope' we don't mean to suggest anything that is uncertain. Hope is a word that has changed its meaning. Hope, in Bible language, equals assurance. The Lord Jesus is our Hope in that although we haven't yet seen Him, we are certain of Him and look forward to the final part of our salvation when we shall see Him and be with Him for ever. 'We rejoice in the hope of the glory of God' (Rom. 5:2).

God's Holy Spirit who lives in us assures us of the glory that is to come (Eph. 1:14). The new birth we've experienced carries with it the certainty that our bodies will share in Jesus' resurrection experience and that we're going to enter into the glorious inheritance He now prepares for us in heaven (1 Pet. 1:3, 4). Citizens as we are of our own nation, we know that our true and lasting citizenship is in heaven. 'And we eagerly await a Saviour from there, the Lord Jesus Christ, who, by the power that enables him to bring everything under his control, will transform our lowly bodies so that they will be like his glorious body' (Phil. 3:20, 21). One of the foremost purposes of our conversion is that we should now wait for Jesus from heaven (1 Thess. 1:10).

Fixing our eyes on the Lord Jesus provides a proper perspective upon life in all its facets. It's all too easy to live as if this world were the only world to be concerned about, and to forget that there's another world in which we ought to be laying up treasures and where the treasures aren't subject to decline in their value or the uncertainties of accident or theft.

It's true that being a Christian is a wonderful experience here and now because it brings us into a right relationship with God and all the joys that flow from that. But being a Christian also brings its own difficulties: we may encounter opposition to our witness, and the tasks to which God calls us may be hard. The devil will often try to whisper to us, 'Is it worth it all? Why not settle for an easy life?' But the assurance of our future salvation is like a helmet to put on our heads (Eph. 6:17; 1 Thess. 5:8), and, as we wear it, Satan's insinuations will fail. We are never more assured of our future salvation, and excited by it, than when we focus our hearts and minds on the Lord Jesus, the secret centre of our lives, seated as He is at the right hand of God for us (Col. 3:1-4).

MAINTAINING OUR FOCUS
Since it's so fundamentally important to fix our eyes on the Lord Jesus, it's not surprising that Satan's principal attacks aim at

sidetracking us from this. He'll seldom employ straightforward ways – he'll try to achieve it by subtle means.

A frequent ruse is his endeavour to encourage us to make a bad thing out of a good thing. For example, Bible study is an essential activity, never to be neglected. But if the devil can get us carried away with the study of the Bible to the neglect of obedience to it so that the study of the Bible becomes an end in itself, then he's won a victory.

It's wonderful when we discover a new truth in the Bible. But here again Satan may be active. Let's imagine that we gain a fresh insight into what the precious gift of the Holy Spirit means to a Christian. That's something for which to be grateful to God. But if the devil can get us to think and talk about nothing else so that we become preoccupied with the Holy Spirit rather than with the Lord Jesus, then the devil has sidetracked us from our proper focus.

We've all cause probably to be grateful for those whom God has used to speak to us – perhaps a Bible teacher, minister or preacher. But if the devil can make our admiration of that person so take hold of us that we talk more about him than about the Lord Jesus Christ, then the devil has won another victory. When John wrote his gospel, one of his purposes was to show that although John the Baptist had been an important witness to the Lord Jesus, that people had got it all wrong when they clung to the witness rather than to Jesus Himself (John 1:6, 7, 8, 15, 19-27, 29-36). The devil has all kinds of ploys to take our eyes off the Lord Jesus, and we're not to be ignorant of the peril.

Awareness of the danger is an important part of the solution to it. Determine that throughout your Christian life – by God's help – the Lord Jesus Christ will be your preoccupation. Make it your ambition to know Him. Be like Paul and recognise everything else as not worth having compared with the surpassing worth of knowing Him (Phil. 3:8).

As you read the Bible day by day, do so with a desire to discover more of the Lord Jesus, and never read it without asking God for the help of the Holy Spirit. His delight is to reveal more of the Lord Jesus to us. He's the secret of the spiritual focus we're able to cultivate in the Christian life.

Whatever else happens, hold fast to the Lord Jesus. Test everything by the place it gives to Him. With your eyes on Him you'll be made radiant and able to cope with everything. If you concentrate on your knowledge of Him, 'You will never fall, and you will receive a rich welcome into the eternal kingdom of our Lord and Saviour Jesus Christ' (2 Pet. 1:10, 11), and then you'll discover how worthwhile it's all been to serve Him!

A PRAYER

Heavenly Father, I delight to call Jesus 'Lord', to Your glory, since You have revealed Yourself to me in Him, and through His death and resurrection I have come to put my faith and hope in You.

Thank You for showing me the central place Your dear Son has in all Your great purposes for the church and for me personally. I rejoice that He is the author and perfecter of my faith and the example of all that You want me to be and do. I would commit myself to make knowing the Lord Jesus my most important objective. May Your Spirit help me to fix my eyes on the Lord Jesus and to set my heart on Him and things above in my heavenly home. Please make me sensitive to anything that detracts me from this spiritual focus and give me the honest ability to deal with it. I want the Lord Jesus to be the chief love of my life and the joy of my heart. I ask it for His Name's sake. Amen.

QUESTIONS

1. Wherever we go in the New Testament the centrality of our Lord Jesus is either openly expressed or implied. Take 1 Corinthians 1:1-9 as an example. How many

truths can you discover about the Lord Jesus Christ from these nine verses?

2. How do you find your focus on the Lord Jesus sometimes threatened? What practical steps can you take with regard to these threats in order to maintain your spiritual focus? Can you think of any good things which the devil has encouraged you to go overboard on, so that they have tended to become a hindrance?

Bible References for Further Study

The supremacy of Jesus in God's purposes:

John 5:39; Acts 2:29-36; 1 Corinthians 15:20-28;
2 Corinthians 1:20; 5:17-21; Ephesians 1:9, 10, 18-23; 3:10-12;
Philippians 2:9-11; Colossians 1:15-20; 2 Thessalonians 2:13, 14;
Titus 2:11-14; Hebrews 1:1-4; 10:12-14; 12:22-24; 13:20, 21;
1 Peter 1:10-12; Revelation 1:17, 18; 5:6-14.

The future aspect of our salvation:

John 11:25, 26; 14:2, 3; 17:24; Romans 8:22-25, 30;
1 Corinthians 15:42-44, 49, 51-54;
2 Corinthians 5:1-5; Philippians 1:23; 3:20, 21;
1 Thessalonians 4:13-18; 2 Thessalonians 1:9, 10; 2:14; 1 John 3:2.

The importance of spiritual focus:

Psalm 16:8; 34:5; 123:1, 2; Matthew 6:33; 2 Corinthians 4:18;
Colossians 3:1-4; 1 Thessalonians 1:10; Hebrews 3:1; 9:28; 11:27;
12:2, 3.

Christian Focus Publications

publishes books for all ages

Our mission statement –

STAYING FAITHFUL

In dependence upon God we seek to impact the world through literature faithful to His infallible Word, the Bible. Our aim is to ensure that the LORD Jesus Christ is presented as the only hope to obtain forgiveness of sin, live a useful life and look forward to heaven with Him.

REACHING OUT

Christ's last command requires us to reach out to our world with His gospel. We seek to help fulfil that by publishing books that point people towards Jesus and help them develop a Christ-like maturity. We aim to equip all levels of readers for life, work, ministry and mission.

Books in our adult range are published in three imprints.

Christian Focus contains popular works including biographies, commentaries, basic doctrine and Christian living. Our children's books are also published in this imprint.

Mentor focuses on books written at a level suitable for Bible College and seminary students, pastors and other serious readers. The imprint includes commentaries, doctrinal studies, examination of current issues and church history.

Christian Heritage contains classic writings from the past.

Christian Focus Publications Ltd,
Geanies House, Fearn, Ross-shire,
IV20 1TW, Scotland, United Kingdom
info@christianfocus.com
www.christianfocus.com